THE CREATIVE CURVE

THE CREATIVE CURVE

HOW TO DEVELOP THE RIGHT IDEA, AT THE RIGHT TIME

ALLEN GANNETT

WH
ALLEN

5 7 9 10 8 6 4

WH Allen, an imprint of Ebury Publishing,
20 Vauxhall Bridge Road,
London SW1V 2SA

WH Allen is part of the Penguin Random House group of companies
whose addresses can be found at global.penguinrandomhouse.com

First published in the United Kingdom by WH Allen in 2018
First published in the United States by Currency in 2018

www.penguin.co.uk

A CIP catalogue record for this book is available from the British Library

ISBN 9780753548738

Printed and bound in Great Britain by Clays Ltd, Elcograf S.p.A.

Book design by Anna Thompson
Illustrations by Greg Fisk

Penguin Random House is committed to a sustainable future
for our business, our readers and our planet. This book is
made from Forest Stewardship Council® certified paper.

MIX
Paper from
responsible sources
FSC® C018179

To Harry Weller

Contents

The Creative Curve

Preface

We've all been told a lie about the nature of creativity.
For as long as anyone can remember, our culture has perpetuated the myth that creative success is the result of a sudden light-bulb moment. That writing bestselling novels, creating revered paintings, or developing viral mobile apps has a mystical quality, unconnected to rational thought or logic, that is reserved for "geniuses" rather than for the rest of us mere mortals.

In fact, for centuries now we have been persuaded of this by wise men and critics who excitedly recount stories of creative genius that emphasize the individual, the subconscious, and the seemingly divine machinations behind creative achievement.

My goal in writing *The Creative Curve* is to reveal the truth about creative success: that there is in fact a science behind what becomes a hit and that today's neuroscience gives us an unprecedented ability to decode and engineer the necessary moments of "inspiration" to create popular work that your audience can't get enough of.

I have always been addicted to patterns. As a kid, this took the form of spending countless hours playing computer games, watching and waiting to see how the AI worked so I could destroy my virtual opponent and save the kingdom (or planet, or country—I think you get the idea). As a teenager, this turned into a short-lived (and fairly successful) obsession with getting cast on game shows.

Today, this lifelong geekery has found two homes.

By day, I run a company that works with large brands to help them uncover the meaning—that is to say, the patterns—within their marketing data. We help Fortune 500s and high-growth start-ups understand the marketing channels, messages, and tactics that will work the best in the future, based on the data from their past.

By night, I've done everything possible to answer the question of whether there is a pattern to creative success. I've spent the last two years interviewing some of the world's most successful creators. From culinary titans to bestselling novelists and even top YouTube Creators, I sat down, ate, chatted, and Skyped with some of the leading so-called creative geniuses of our time. In addition, I spoke to the most distinguished academics in the studies of creativity, genius, and neuroscience.

What did I find?

It turns out that the mythology around creativity is just that, myth. You do not have to be born with some X-Men-like superpower to achieve great artistic or entrepreneurial heights. In fact, there *is* a pattern that successful creative people leverage to make hits, one that's accessible to almost anyone. It's intuitive, but it's also learnable. And it has nothing to do with mysticism. You don't need to take LSD to get inspired, or pray for a moment of overwhelming insight.

Based on what I found, it turns out you can *intentionally* follow what the world's most vaunted creative geniuses do—and get that much closer to creating and executing your *own* great ideas.

Let's get started.

Part I

Overturning the Mythology of Creativity

The Making of a Dream

I t was November 1963.

Paul McCartney woke up obsessed with a melody he had heard while dreaming. The twenty-one-year-old pop star stumbled over to the small piano nestled in his room on the top floor of 57 Wimpole Street in central London.

What was that melody?

He sat at the piano, trying to re-create the notes he had heard in his sleep.

It felt so familiar.

He finally put it together: G, F-sharp minor 7th, B, E minor, and E. He played it again and again. He loved the way it sounded but was certain the melody must come from some half-forgotten song he had heard before. Like many musicians, he fretted that he might be borrowing the melody of another song. *Too familiar*, he thought. *Where have I heard this before?*

The melody McCartney heard in his dream would ultimately become "Yesterday," the most recorded song in music history, with three thousand different versions. It has been played more than seven million times on American television and radio and is the fourth-highest-grossing song of all time.

McCartney himself once said of his famous song, "It is possibly the smash of this century." Indeed, "Yesterday" may well have been one of the twentieth century's biggest hits, and, apparently, it was the result of a dream. He told an interviewer for *The Beatles Anthology* that the experience had a profound impact on how he viewed creativity: "It's amazing that it just came to me in a dream. That's why I don't profess to know anything; I think music is all very mystical."

For creativity researchers, Paul McCartney's sudden melodic epiphany is a classic example of creativity coming to an artist unplanned, in a flash of genius: a "moment of inspiration," in which an idea suddenly rises to one's conscious awareness. It is the unexpected nature of these bursts of inspiration, with no apparent origin, that gives them a supernatural quality. Anyone who has had a great idea in the shower or on a run or walk has experienced some version of these moments.

Whether it is J. K. Rowling being struck with the idea for Harry Potter on a train to London, or Mozart being able to compose songs without effort, these accounts have become modern-day staples of what I call the *inspiration theory of creativity*: the idea that creative success results from a mysterious internal process punctuated by unpredictable flashes of genius. And our culture has embraced the idea that a self-reliant person, born with the right innate talents, can produce hits out of sheer inspiration.

What's more, this view is not confined to the traditional arts, like music and literature. Steve Jobs, the prototypical genius of the digital age, explained, in an often-repeated quote, that creativity is an organic process: "When you ask creative people how they did something, they feel a little guilty because they didn't really *do* it, they just *saw* something."

The inspiration theory of creativity dominates how most people think about creative greatness today. But why do these sudden moments of inspiration occur? Is sheer IQ genius the only explanation? If we studied the settings of these creative moments, would they verify or disprove the inspiration theory?

Name That Tune

The morning the melody for "Yesterday" came to McCartney was a typical lazy day. As was his routine, he awoke around noon. He and his girlfriend Jane would often stay out late at London's restaurants and clubs.

McCartney worried about why the melody he woke up with was so clear, so concise. It seemed too finished, too complete. He assumed he had accidently plagiarized it. Was it from one of the classics he had heard his father play so often? "Stairway to Paradise"? "Chicago"? "Lullaby of the Leaves"?

The Beatles were thoughtful about creating their hits. Lennon once described to an interviewer how intentional the band had been when writing their first number-one single, "Please Please Me": "We tried to make it as simple as possible . . . we aimed this one straight at the hit parade. It was my attempt at writing a Roy Orbison song."

For McCartney, "Yesterday" was an explicit exception to his typical methodical songwriting process. The tune of "Yesterday" was like "a jazz melody," McCartney later said. "My dad used to know a lot of old jazz tunes. I thought maybe I'd just remembered it from the past."

He went to his friends and asked if they recognized the song.

First, he asked his songwriting partner, John Lennon. Lennon told him he had never heard it before. Still skeptical, McCartney tried his friend Lionel Bart, who had composed numerous hit songs. When McCartney hummed the melody, Bart drew a blank. It seemed as if the song might be original.

Still not convinced, McCartney pressed on. He tried to think of someone older and more experienced, someone who might be able to clear his conscience.

A few days later, McCartney visited Alma Cogan, a British singer known for the song "Dreamboat" and sixteen other hits. If anyone could recognize the song, she could.

He sat down at the piano and played the melody for Cogan and her sister. "It's lovely," Cogan said when he was done.

Had she heard it before? McCartney asked. Was it someone else's song?

Cogan said, "No. It's original. Nice song."

Finally, McCartney was persuaded. He had seemingly dreamed a masterful melody, following the mystical nature of the inspiration theory of creativity.

We can interpret the inspiration theory in one of two ways.

The positive view is that a flash of genius can strike anyone. "Yesterday" came to McCartney in a dream, outside of his control. It's possible that all of us can dream a chart-topping melody.

On the other hand, most of us believe that if we lack the raw talent or innate genius, these moments will never strike. The inspiration theory of creativity is only relevant for those born with so-called genius.

As a result, many of us are tempted to put aside any ambition to become the next great musician, novelist, or entrepreneur, settling instead to be a consumer or patron of the arts. Meanwhile, the optimistic ones are just waiting, hoping for a sudden flash of inspiration to visit them.

The inspiration theory is supported by countless anecdotes from the creative artists of our time. Authors talk of waiting for creative inspiration. Entrepreneurs talk of waiting for a great idea to strike. Musicians talk of falling into a creative groove.

There are countless books and blog posts on creativity, offering suggestions on how we can push through writer's block or discover our "flow." Biopics of great artists amplify the inevitability

THE MAKING OF A DREAM / 7

of their creativity, as well as suggesting it is the domain of mad geniuses.

Meanwhile, the rest of us are left on the sidelines.

But what if this entire theory is wrong? What if you don't have to wait for lightning to strike?

The Road to "Yesterday"

While the sudden creation story of "Yesterday" is relatively well known, what is less known is how McCartney went from the original melody to crafting the full song.

The notion that this song came to McCartney in an instant is wrong.

All that had come to him in the dream was a simple chord progression. When McCartney awoke with a melody in his head, it was a long way from a completed song. For one thing, the tune had no words. He knew he needed to come up with placeholder lyrics while he continued working on the song's structure.

As he was playing the melody to Alma Cogan, her mother walked into the room, asking, "Anyone like some scrambled eggs?"

This gave McCartney the temporary lyric he needed: Scrambled Eggs.

The initial lyrics he came up with were:

Scrambled eggs
Oh, my baby, how I love your legs
Diddle diddle
I believe in scrambled eggs.

From there, it took almost twenty months of grueling work to complete the song. McCartney became obsessed. While he worked on it, the people around McCartney became sick of hearing about his ever-changing song in progress.

As George Harrison told an interviewer about that period, "He's always talking about that song. You'd think he was Beethoven or somebody . . ."

Even when the Beatles started filming their second movie, *Help!*, McCartney didn't waver. He worked on the song during breaks. At one point, the film's producer, Dick Lester, was so fed up that he said, "If you play that bloody song any longer, I'll have the piano taken offstage. Either finish it, or give it up!"

Later, on their first tour through France, Paul had a piano placed in their hotel room so that he could continue working on "Yesterday." It paid off. When producer George Martin first heard the song, he was mesmerized. It was different. In fact, it was *so* original that he was worried that it wouldn't fit into a Beatles album.

McCartney realized that the song needed melancholy lyrics (scrambled eggs were not a valid topic for a brooding song). "I remember thinking that people liked sad tunes; they like to wallow a bit when they're alone, to put a record on and go, 'Ahh.'" He finally finished the song, sketching out the final lyrics, on a trip to Portugal in May 1965.

A month later he went to the studio with George Martin to record "Yesterday." According to Martin, McCartney came into Studio Two at EMI and played "Yesterday" on an acoustic guitar. The only change Martin could think of was adding orchestral strings. Paul, however, thought that was too much. In response, Martin suggested a quartet, and with that melodic but dark addition, "Yesterday" was born.

The iconic song that is remembered as the result of a flash of genius was, in fact, a nearly two-year odyssey—one that at times wore McCartney (and his friends) down. While the mythology behind the Beatles celebrates the story of "Yesterday" as one of sudden creative genius, as we've seen it was hardly a linear path from dream to recording. "Yesterday" was not a pure product of a light-bulb moment. It was hard, grueling work.

But couldn't you argue that it began with an initial moment of divine inspiration? How do we account for that?

There is a cottage industry of researchers who are fascinated by the origin story of "Yesterday": academics interested in creativity, music historians, and avid Beatles fans. All have worked to answer the question of where the melody *really* came from.

The most enlightening theory of the origin of "Yesterday" comes from Beatles expert Ian Hammond, who points out that the song "is a direct evolution of the melody from the Ray Charles version of 'Georgia on My Mind.' Not only does 'Yesterday' share a chord progression with the earlier song, but it also mirrors the bass lines of 'Georgia on My Mind.'"

True enough, the Beatles and Paul McCartney were big admirers of Ray Charles. They kicked off their career playing his covers in the bars and clubs of Hamburg, Germany. John Lennon said that when they started playing their own songs, it was a "quite traumatic thing because we were doing such great numbers of other people's, of Ray Charles and [Little] Richard and all of them."

For Paul McCartney, what looked like divine inspiration was in fact likely the result of subconscious processing of music he loved. Like most music, it was an evolution of the chord progressions that already existed. In fact, as Hammond points out, Ray Charles's version of "Georgia on My Mind" was an evolution of Hoagy Carmichael's original version of the song. This type of ingestion, reinvention, and influence is common in stories of creative success.

When McCartney reflects on how he wrote "Yesterday," he tends to focus on his sudden inspiration for the tune. But, in at least one interview, he acknowledged that there was something more mechanical at work: "If you're very spiritual then God sent me a melody, I'm a mere vehicle. If you wanna be a bit more cynical, then I was loading my computer for millions of years listening to all the stuff I listened to through my dad and through my musical tastes, including people like Fred Astaire, Gershwin, and finally my computer printed out one morning what it thought was a good tune."

The things we view as unexplainable genius often have a genesis of some sort.

The inspiration theory of creativity has been around for thousands of years, since the era of ancient Greece. While the theory is still breathlessly recounted in the press, modern research that I'll discuss demonstrates that creative potential is within all of us.

However, if our perception of McCartney and other creative artists is flawed—if they are more accurately described as tireless and intensely focused—that still does not explain how they achieved commercial success. Plenty of artists toil away for years at their craft without recognition or acclaim. An endless procession of novelists *has* labored tirelessly for years writing novels that never sell a copy. Many painters, sculptors, choreographers, and musicians work for years without ever tasting critical or commercial success. Clearly, popular success is not just a matter of sweat equity.

Could it be possible to identify the true causes of creative success?

Learning a Lie

As I said earlier, I have always been addicted to recognizing patterns. Much of the phenomena we observe that seem organic or unique are actually the result of repeating processes and systems. By decoding the right patterns, I believe you can achieve goals ranging from the frivolous to the meaningful.

When I was eighteen, I set my sights on getting on a game show. It seemed like an unusual challenge, yet one that offered a potentially fun and lucrative reward. So, I applied to all the shows I had heard of (and some I hadn't known existed).

Some asked for essays. Others, like *Jeopardy*, asked you to take online tests. Still others, like *Wheel of Fortune*, simply requested you fill out a form.

I sent away e-mails and filled out web forms, and then I waited.

After months of not hearing anything, one day an e-mail appeared asking me to audition for *Wheel of Fortune*. Rather than study the puzzles, I decided I would spend the weeks before my audition trying to figure out what the producers wanted. I watched dozens of episodes, looking for common elements in the contestants' behavior. I delved through message boards about how the game worked and read blog posts about other peoples' experiences auditioning. After hours of research, I found a pattern: the casting team wasn't looking for expert puzzle-solvers. They were seeking contestants who could enunciate (and really loudly, too), were willing to embarrass themselves, and who came across to a home audience as over-the-top and energetic.

That's why instead of studying vocab words, I came up with various ways I could embarrass myself. I worked on an Elmo impression that I thought might make the audience laugh—or cringe—and on the morning of my audition, I drank two shots of espresso. A lack of energy would not be an obstacle.

It worked! That year I was cast on *Wheel of Fortune*. While I lost to Joanne from Virginia—I really should have studied the puzzles—I now had a hypothesis: Television producers were looking for a particular type of individual with energy whom, with practice, I could emulate.

I wanted to prove to myself that my success at getting cast was repeatable and not a fluke, so I auditioned for another game show.

A few months later, I was cast on MTV's *Movers and Changers*, a cheesy business competition hosted by Nick Cannon. The show was similar to what *Shark Tank* would later become, and again, I lost. My business idea was judged by some well-known personalities like CNBC's Jim Cramer, who voted me off the proverbial island, or as he would say, *sell, sell, sell!*

Eventually my preoccupation with patterns led to more serious endeavors.

While this book is not a marketing book (although marketers *will* be able to apply these concepts), many of my observations grew out of my frustrations as a marketer. In 2011, I had become a CMO of a venture-backed start-up, and I wanted to improve our performance. Once again, I sought out patterns. I pored through our campaign and audience analytics, and lo and behold, I ended up with data that revealed how we could improve our efforts. I was able to uncover the topics and tactics that resonated with our audience. However, finding these patterns took hours of manual work and was incredibly tedious.

So in 2012, I quit my job and founded TrackMaven, a company that provides predictive analytics to marketers. I wanted to automate what I had been doing before with spreadsheets and Excel formulas.

Some of the world's biggest brands now hire TrackMaven to decode their marketing data. Our software is built on the premise that if you look at millions of pieces of marketing content from a brand, you'll find patterns that answer valuable questions. Should the financial services company invest in more Facebook advertising? What is better for the retail brand to talk about on its blog: discounts or new items? Is there an ideal number of e-mails a company should send before customers start pressing the Unsubscribe button? Our platform makes it straightforward for companies to answer these questions.

Since its founding, the company has been in growth overdrive. We have raised more than $28 million in institutional capital, have worked with hundreds of companies ranging from the Fortune 500s to high-growth start-ups, and were named one of the fastest growing companies in America according to the Inc. 500.

Since we ingest data from some of the world's biggest brands, we see data that no one else sees.

With this unique perspective, I found another surprising pattern: Most marketers are failing.

Marketing is supposed to be one of the most creative parts of business. Yet according to the Content Marketing Institute, only 30 percent of consumer marketers believe that their content works. Another study found that only 2.8 percent of business-to-business marketing campaigns achieved their targets. Failure has become the status quo for most marketers. Why, I asked, are some of the most creative people in organizations failing?

To answer this question, I went on the road to meet with numerous marketers. I wanted to understand why they were more often than not coming up short. Were they creating too much content? Too little? How could the statistics around success be so uniformly negative?

What I found was that today's marketers are following the wrong patterns. They tend to use words like *innovation, collaboration,* and *brainstorming.* To me, that is really industry-speak for a group of people waiting around for a light-bulb moment. Like those who believe in the inspiration myth, they believe great campaign ideas will simply strike them at the right time.

Marketers are unconsciously following the traditional myth of the inspiration theory of creativity in their careers and in their offices.

What do I mean by that? They design the layout of their offices to foster brainstorming. Conference rooms and whiteboards are scattered everywhere, as if their mere presence might unleash pent-up creativity. According to one trade group, almost 70 percent of all offices are now designed as open spaces meant to encourage collaboration and cross-pollination. And sure, companies and teams are brainstorming more than ever before. Nevertheless, across the board, most marketers' content does not become viral or ignite sales.

Clearly, the open-office plans and whiteboard bonanza are not fostering a new era of creativity.

Nor is that approach just embraced by marketers. I met with creators from all backgrounds and trades, from painters to chefs to writers to entrepreneurs. I found that across every creative discipline, people have adopted the inspiration theory of creativity as their model for finding (stumbling upon, really) mainstream success. The writers I know, the entrepreneurs I know, even the artists I know, try to optimize for moments of sudden brilliance. But even with all the focus on brainstorming and inspiration, most novels fail, most start-ups go bankrupt, and most artists never take off. Throughout creative fields, the most followed pattern of creativity, one of free association and free-flowing thought, is falling short.

Worse, too many people with passion, buying into the notion that creativity is the province of geniuses, give up even trying to be creators. They abandon their dreams and become consumers of culture, rather than creators of it. A recent global study of five thousand people found that only 25 percent believe they are fulfilling their creative potential.

On the other hand, there are a handful of creative geniuses, from Pablo Picasso to Steve Jobs, who *do* achieve large-scale commercial success.

How do they do it? And why are the results for most of us so bad? Are these creative geniuses born with an instinct for turning ideas into things to be revered? Are they just lucky, or is there something beyond our understanding at play? Do most of us have no chance at achieving mainstream success?

To answer these questions, I decided to reverse engineer creative success. What does it take to create a hit, whether a hit restaurant, a hit screenplay, or a popular poem? Is there a pattern? Is creative success something you can practice, hone, and enhance?

I tackled the problem by going right to the source. I spoke with people who had reached the pinnacle of creative and commercial achievement. I wanted to uncover what the world's most successful people did to unlock their potential, even if they couldn't put exact words to it. Flying around the world to meet painters and chefs, Skyping with rock stars and entrepreneurs, I interviewed dozens of creative geniuses on their process, asking about their childhoods, their brainstorming process, and even the layouts of their workspaces. I wanted to see if I could find any dots that would connect. I met these people through a variety of circumstances. Sometimes it was as simple as reaching out to them via e-mail. I contacted others through layers of managers. And many were introduced through mutual connections.

I also devoured the latest science on creativity, interviewing academics who are using the latest tools and technologies to decode genius, and poring over thousands of pages of peer-reviewed articles and journals. I wanted to learn if science could help us explain what it takes to create a hit.

What was the result of my investigation? Not only did I discover the hidden patterns I was looking for, I learned something surprising and exciting: *that the inspiration theory of creativity simply isn't true.*

In fact, as I will show, studies prove that the majority of us are born with the same creative potential as artists who create hit after hit. I also learned that there is an evolutionary basis for what commands dollars and attention; that successful ideas are not born of mysterious origins; and that what we think of as flashes of genius are actually a biological process that anyone can cultivate. In short, I learned that there is a science and a method to achieving mainstream success, one that anyone can work to master.

In this book, I will walk you through the patterns I found.

This is not a marketing book. It is not a self-help book. It is, simply, a guide to understanding the patterns of creativity that result in breakthrough success. You will learn the history of creative thought and how it has developed from the time of the Greeks to today's fast-paced world of Snapchat and Instagram. You will discover the neuroscience that underpins the creation of trends. Finally, you will uncover the four patterns that successful creative people follow to increase their odds of achieving mainstream success, and you will understand the science that explains *why* they work. As you will find out, while this is a conscious process for some, most creators follow these patterns *unconsciously* as the result of similar methods of early instruction and learning.

A word of caution. The standard academic definition of creativity is the ability to make something that is *novel*, and that also has *value*. It is a mistake to think that creativity is just about creating something different or original. It also has to be valuable, meaning that a group of people, large or small, have found importance or usefulness in that creative product. A pop star who creates a hit song has created something novel and of value. An entrepreneur who creates a viral app is worthy of study. This means that my exploration will *not* just be focused on the traditional painters and artists you might see at the Getty Museum or the Louvre. While I will talk about many of those traditional creators, I will also include numerous contemporary artists, entrepreneurs, creative individuals, and companies ranging from singer/songwriter Taylor Swift to the flavor team at Ben & Jerry's.

As a result, I'll also dive into the science of trends. Trends signify that a large group of people agrees that something—a song, product, or idea—has value. As far as trends are concerned, research identifies two seemingly contradictory urges in the human psyche: People crave the familiar, yet seek the novel. To protect ourselves from the unknown, we seek the familiar—for example, the comfort of our home or the company of close friends. We also seek the stimulation and potential rewards of novel and unusual things. Anyone who has wanted to try a new restaurant or listen to a new song knows what I am talking about.

Studies show that the tension between these contradictory urges creates a bell-shaped curve relationship between preference and familiarity. As individuals or groups are exposed to something, they like it more and more with each additional exposure until it reaches a peak of popularity. At that point it becomes overexposed, and each additional exposure leads to lower popularity.

The Creative Curve

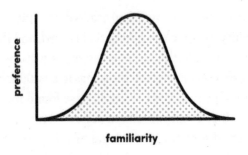

I call this bell-shaped curve the *creative curve*.

Sociologists, psychologists, and economists have known about—and have been writing about—these contradictory urges, and the bell-shaped curve they produce, for decades. In his 1967 book *Man's Rage for Chaos*, Morse Peckham explained how this paradox drives our cultural aesthetic. Almost fifty years later, Jonah Berger's 2016 book, *Invisible Influence*, described how ideas that are "similar, but different" have the most social influence. Even more recently, Derek Thompson's book *Hit Makers* describes how twentieth-century industrial designers observed this phenomenon in a principal called "Most Advanced Yet Acceptable."

What nobody has described, however, is how to find the sweet spot on the creative curve, the point of optimal tension between preference and familiarity, safety and surprise, similarity and difference. In the course of my interviews and research, I discovered that popular creators consciously or unconsciously have developed a method for doing just this, whether they are able to articulate it or not. What is called creative genius is really the ability to understand the mechanics of the creative curve and use it to engineer mainstream success.

Regardless of the industries they work in, the innovators I interviewed make use of shockingly similar methods. They understand what is familiar and use novelty in ways they know their audience will respond to. They then slowly change their artistic style to drive continued interest in their work.

The methods these creators have learned to master the creative curve are what I call the *laws of the creative curve*. In the course of the book, I will outline and explain these four laws: the *law of consumption*, the *law of imitation*, the *law of creative communities*, and the *law of iterations*.

Creative geniuses consistently outperform the rest of society by either subconsciously or consciously utilizing the laws of the creative curve to develop a scalable system of success that helps them discover or create ideas that combine just the right blend of familiar and novel.

For each law, I will explain the scientific thinking that underlies it, as well as offer practical examples of how to use it. The good news is that these laws can apply to any creative field or creative person.

Again, the traditional view of creativity implies that we all exist in a world of infinite possibilities, and must wait for a novel idea to cut through the noise. We are told that serendipitous moments can occur unpredictably, anytime, while we're in the shower, on our commute, or in the boardroom.

In this book, I will disprove this, and I will break down the science behind the creative curve, providing you with a methodology that will enable you to maximize your odds of creating a hit—no matter the industry.

3

The Origin of the Myth

The inspiration theory of creativity suggests that creativity is a mysterious internal process, roiling and churning inside us, punctuated by flashes of insight that bubble to the surface without warning. In short, creativity, as most of us have come to understand it, is a random gift from God. However, there are two additional elements of the inspiration theory: first, that you have to be a traditional, or "IQ," genius to be struck by great creative ideas, and second, that it helps to be a little bit neurotic or manic. In other words, creative brilliance is innate–we're born with it, or we aren't, and being a bit "different" tends to come with it.

You will often see this theory highlighted in our entertainment. It was on full display in the movie adaptation of *Amadeus*, which won eight Academy Awards in 1985, including Best Picture.

Amadeus depicts Wolfgang Amadeus Mozart's bristling relationship with Antonio Salieri, who saw himself as Mozart's rival. The movie shows a blindfolded Mozart as a child playing piano flawlessly to kings and popes. It claims that Mozart, a prodigy with mesmerizing talent, composed his first concerto at four years old.

In the film, Salieri toils relentlessly on his compositions, re-working them again and again. When he discovers that Mozart, now a young man, creates impeccable first drafts with no sign of editing or revisions, he is furious.

In one scene, Salieri gazes at a finished Mozart composition: "Astounding! It was actually beyond belief. These were first and only drafts of music, yet they showed no corrections of any kind. . . . Here again was the very voice of God!"

Salieri was both awestruck and envious. Divine music seemed to just flow out of Mozart. What's more, Mozart, at least as he was portrayed in the film, was an immature drunk who didn't take himself seriously.

Many of us consider Mozart to be the embodiment of the inspiration theory of creativity. Famed movie critic Roger Ebert said that *Amadeus*'s characterization of Mozart was "not a vulgarization of Mozart, but a way of dramatizing that true geniuses rarely take their own work seriously, because it comes so easily for them."

The film's portrayal has its origins in a letter written by Mozart that was published in 1815 by a leading German music magazine.

The magazine's publisher was an avid fan of and expert on the composer, telling all who would listen stories about how Mozart would compose in his head, without benefit of a piano.

In the letter, Mozart explained his composition process: "Provided I am not disturbed, my subject enlarges itself, becomes methodized and defined, and the whole, though it be long, stands almost finished and complete in my mind, so that I can survey it, like a fine picture or a beautiful statue, at a glance. Nor do I hear in my imagination the parts successively, but I hear them, as it were, all at once."

This letter became a cornerstone of the mythology that grew around Mozart: the brilliant composer did not toil for his musical ideas; he was handed them by a mysterious Higher Power. This account, like countless other popular stories that refer to flashes of genius, can be enough to dissuade any aspiring individual who is not convinced they are a genius connected to God to give up his creative efforts. If you're not born with a once-in-a-generation gift, you don't stand a chance of making your mark.

There is one problem with Mozart's letter: It was a forgery.

The portrait of Mozart's inspired brilliance came about as the result of an overly ambitious publisher trying to sell magazines. Johann Rochlitz was a German magazine publisher who had a deep reverence for Mozart and published countless letters and anecdotes that were purportedly from or about Mozart. However, later biographers discovered that many of his stories were exaggerated, and some, such as this letter, were wholly fabricated.

Nevertheless, the myth took hold. A few hundred years later, this conception of Mozart is still deeply ingrained in our consciousness.

In reality, Mozart worked long hours in a highly iterative, backbreaking process. He described a set of string quartets he composed as the "fruit of long and laborious effort." Mozart would create numerous sketches, the music composer's equivalent of rough drafts, as he worked through the various parts of his compositions.

Mozart even used a type of shorthand for drafting that made it easier for him to edit his work.

The idea that Mozart composed pieces entirely in his head was also not true. In his actual letters, he makes it very clear that he wrote at a keyboard, as he needed to hear the notes as he was working.

Another aspect of the Mozart myth was that he was a child prodigy, born with unprecedented gifts. According to Salieri in *Amadeus*, Mozart composed his first concertos at the age of four. In reality, the first piano concerto he "wrote" was at age eleven, after years of daily focused practice insisted upon by his father. But these first pieces, it turns out, were *not* actually original, but instead were reinterpretations of others' songs. His father began training Mozart in music when he was three years old, and Mozart's first truly *original* concerto was written when he was seventeen years old. This may still seem young, but at that point Mozart had almost fourteen years of intense practice behind him. Fourteen years of long, daily practice is not the same as being simply *born* a world-class composer.

Finally, Mozart and Salieri were actually friends! Yes, they sometimes competed for jobs, but, outside of friendly competition, they enjoyed each other's company, composed a piece together—*Per la ricuperata salute di Ofelia*—and Salieri was, in fact, Mozart's son's music *teacher* for a time!

Mozart, an early standard-bearer for the inspiration theory of creativity, was, in fact, a practitioner of intense and diligent effort.

Yet the inspiration theory of creativity shows up not just in pop culture and films, but also in mainstream media and academia.

The *New York Times* columnist David Brooks, in a 2016 piece about creativity, argues that "inspiration is not something you can control." He does not believe it is merely the result of hard work. "People who are inspired have lost some agency," Brooks goes on. "They often feel that something is working through them, some power greater than themselves. The Greeks said it was the Muses. Believers might say it is God or the Holy Spirit. Others might say it is something mysterious bursting forth deep in the unconscious, a new way of seeing."

Brooks suggests that such inspiration is beyond comprehension.

This idea that creativity is something somewhat mystical runs rampant through Western civilization. Academic researchers seem especially obsessed with the idea that genius is some superior form of humanity. A review of Ph.D. dissertations on the topic of creativity found that six out of ten focused on it as an individual phenomenon.

Yet, as we'll see, this aspect of the inspiration theory of creativity, too, is a myth. Like Mozart's forged letter, it has been embellished and amplified by critics for hundreds of years. To recap, there are four main elements of this myth. First, it is an individual act—the domain of the "solo genius" born with these talents.

Second, that moments of brilliance come as sudden epiphanies that overtake the creator (such as with the creation of "Yesterday"). Third, that once overtaken by inspiration, success comes easily. Fourth and finally, creative people, like Mozart, are somewhat mad, neurotic, or manic—and often all three!

As you'll see, these ideas are either exaggerated or worse—as with Mozart—made up. But where do these ideas even come from? If they're not true, why have so many come to believe the inspiration myth? And what is the actual truth about creative talent?

The History of Creativity

"A poet is a light and winged thing, and holy, and never able to compose until he has become inspired, and is beside himself, and reason is no longer in him." If you believe this is another David Brooks quote you're only off by a couple thousand years. Plato said it.

Much of our modern perspective on creativity goes all the way back to the early Greeks.

Plato considered an artist to be one who imitated the reality that God created. In fact, the word that the Greeks used to describe an artist's work is *mimesis*, which means "to imitate."

Plato expanded on this view of artists, saying, "These lovely poems are not of man or human workmanship, but are divine and from the gods, and that poets are nothing but interpreters of the gods, each one possessed by the divinity to whom he is in bondage."

Plato and the Greeks provide the historical underpinning for the idea that a creative person is a possessed soul channeling ideas from the gods. The Latin term for *genius* meant a spirit that possesses and protects an individual, a concept that transferred over to the Greeks.

The Greeks also introduced the idea that artists are different from the rest of us. Plato calls the state that poets enter "delirium." Aristotle, too, picks up this same refrain, saying that when mania strikes, "many persons become poets, prophets, and sibyls [fortune tellers], and . . . are pretty good poets while they are maniacal; but when cured can no longer write verse." Genius, it seemed, was intertwined with madness.

The Greeks therefore provided a handful of ideas essential to the inspiration theory of creativity: artists were divinely inspired, and the result of a manic spiritual possession. The role of an artist continued to develop throughout the ages.

Visiting Medieval Times

Today great artists are heralded in museums and galleries. Auction houses sell famous works for hundreds of thousands, if not millions, of dollars. However, in the medieval view of creativity, the artist was merely an imitator, copying God's reality. Accordingly, early Western society viewed artists as mere craftspeople. Over a phone call, Professor Deborah Haynes, who has written numerous art history books, told me these early artists were ranked in the social order below merchants and only a rung above slaves.

There was no concept of a "famous artist." Most pieces of art were unsigned. In part, this was because art was typically a collective effort, created in workshops. What's more, most of the work artists created was not original. Instead, artists followed strict guidelines by imitating the recurring political and religious art required by churches and civic organizations.

Artists were skilled workers, nothing more divine than that. They would be analogous to today's trained carpenters or bricklayers.

But as time went on, and European countries prospered through trading, the market for art exploded. A rising class of merchants was eager to spend their wealth and live like kings, rich noblemen still wanted to decorate their palaces, and churches continued to want awe-inspiring frescos and sculptures.

This increased hunger for art resulted in two significant changes in the Western art world.

First, the interest in their work gave artists a small taste of power. Emboldened, they began engaging in collective bargaining. They joined guilds, an early form of unions, which mandated working conditions, tools, costs, and even techniques. These guilds elevated the artist to a higher place in the social pecking order.

However, according to Deborah Haynes, as individual artists began to prosper they began to split off from the guilds and work directly for the new patronage class.

The newfound wealth of the patrons, and their insatiable desire for art, led to the onset of the Italian Renaissance. Very soon there emerged the notion of the artist as an individual. For the first time there were even *famous* artists, men such as Leonardo da Vinci and Michelangelo. As their work became more coveted, artists pushed for the culture to view them as superior—almost heroic—individuals. The patrons were willing to oblige, and for the first time established artists were seen as creative geniuses (with egos to match).

A Pope and a Brothel

A Vatican official was aghast as he looked up at the fresco painted by Michelangelo on the altar of the Sistine Chapel. The painting depicted God's final judgment after Jesus' Second Coming. Yet unlike most religious paintings of the time, many people in this painting were proudly naked. Nude caricatures were not unprecedented, but typically they would be portrayed as somewhat ashamed of their nudity.

The Last Judgement is one of the most important works of the

Italian Renaissance. Nonetheless, Biagio da Cesena, an aide to the pope, told people it was a work suited for a wall in a "bagnio," or brothel.

Michelangelo was incensed by Biagio's criticism. He alone had decided to strip the saints, and he would not be bullied by some bureaucrat. He decided to take revenge by adding a figure to the painting: Biagio the official portrayed as Minos, the judge of the dead. What's more, in the painting the figure based on Biagio had a snake wrapped around him not once, but twice, symbolizing that he was in the second circle of Hell, or where Dante would put the lustful and perverse. In a final rebuke, the snake was painted in such a way that it appeared to be gnawing on Biagio's genitals.

Not surprisingly, Biagio was furious. Who did this Michelangelo think he was? Biagio complained directly to the pope, but the pope refused to intervene. According to one account, the pope told Biagio, "My authority does not extend into hell."

Michelangelo was demonstrating the newfound power of the celebrity artists, capable of standing up to high-ranking religious officials.

This story has been handed down through history thanks in part to Giorgio Vasari, a writer during the Italian Renaissance who penned one of the first works of art history, an encyclopedia of Italian artists, with brief biographical sketches. It helped to canonize the included artists.

In his book, Vasari also defines the Renaissance view of creativity. He explains that while the ancient Greeks saw artists as simply copying God's work, and medieval rulers believed that artists were mere craftsmen, the Renaissance culture believed that artists weren't just copying God, they were actually *Godlike*. "And the master, that divine light infused by special grace into us, which has not only made us superior to the other animals, but, if it be not sin to say it, like to God."

No longer did only God "create," but artists "created" things as well. In addition, the Renaissance philosophers, and specifically Vasari, began to establish a link between intelligence and creativity. Whereas earlier thinkers viewed artists as lowly craftspeople whose job descriptions could best be summarized as "imitating," Vasari focuses on the intelligence of great artists. Of one great painter he writes, "Although he applied himself to the art of painting very late, when already grown up, nevertheless, he was so well assisted by nature, which inclined him to this, and by his intelligence, which was very beautiful, that soon he produced therein marvellous fruits." This pervasive thinking led to artists migrating from learning in workshops to studying in prestigious art academies, the first of which was created by Vasari himself with the financial backing of Duke Medici.

Not only were artists now fiercely intelligent Godlike creators, some artists even *improved* on reality with their art. The English Renaissance expanded on this line of thinking. The poet Philip Sidney wrote, "Nature never set forth the earth in so rich tapestry as divers [sic] poets have done." However, the artist was still viewed as mad. Shakespeare wrote, "The lunatic, the lover and the poet / Are of imagination all compact."

Artists had become like gods, albeit somewhat neurotic and manic (you can rejoice if you have ever been described as such).

Of Monsters and Men

"We will each write a ghost story!"

George Gordon Byron, the twenty-eight-year-old famed Romantic poet, had cabin fever. Huddled at his lake house, Byron and his friends had spent the summer of 1816 surrounded by rain and darkness thanks to a volcanic eruption, which had turned winter into a twelve-month season, and the trip to the lakeside had devolved into countless hours stuck inside the house. To kill time, George and his friends had started reading aloud a book of German ghost stories. It was under these conditions that George laid out his challenge—that each them write a ghost story. Among them was eighteen-year-old Mary, the lover of another cabin guest, Percy. Mary and Percy had run off two years earlier and had been traveling the world. Her parents were both well-known literary giants, but she was still trying to find her way in the world. As she sat beside Percy, she was stumped. What kind of ghost story could she write?

Hours turned to days. George and Percy both started piecing together their ghoulish tales. Percy would ask Mary about her progress, but she had nothing. One day she overheard Percy and George talking about a recent scientific finding. A botanist had claimed to observe microscopic animals that continued to move, seemingly after their own deaths. The men talked about the idea of a human corpse coming back to life. With all the scientific advancement of the day, it did not seem impossible.

The conversation was all Mary needed to start writing her ghost story, and soon she had a short story completed. Encouraged by the feedback she got, the story eventually grew into a novel that she published anonymously two years later. She named the novel *Frankenstein*.

Mary Wollstonecraft Shelley was only twenty years old when her book was published, yet the young writer had created a gripping tale that has survived for generations. Her story, again, is based on a stereotype of the creative genius, a brilliant scientist who goes mad and uses his expertise to create a monster.

Shelley was part of the English Romantic movement. The Romantics believed that geniuses were mad, and born with an innate talent that allowed them to create paintings, poems, and works of literature. Godlike, but somewhat crazy, they were able to create whole worlds with their paintbrushes and pencils.

This idea of the "mad genius" continued into the Victorian era. In the late 1850s, Charles Darwin published his book *On the Origin* of Species by Means of Natural Selection, which among other things led to an effort to understand the scientific and evolutionary roots of creativity and genius. In fact, Victorian scholars wrote numerous books on the scientific origins of the so-called mad genius in books that captured mainstream attention, including Hereditary Genius, Man of Genius, and Insanity of Genius (seemingly, they lacked original titles).

The second of these, Man of Genius, published in 1891, sought to prove the interconnection between genius and insanity. The author, Cesare Lombroso, uses tenuous logic, claiming that "the fact, now unquestioned, that certain great men of genius have been insane, permits us to presume the existence of a lesser degree of psychosis in other men of genius."

His evidence is often nonsensical. For example, he highlights that artists are often short and pale. And in what must have been a revelation to him, he adds that geniuses have "a tendency to puns and plays upon words."

Where did he think these "disturbing" traits came from?

Hereditary degeneration—where underfunctioning mental or physical conditions in parents are passed down to their children genetically. According to Lombroso, these inherited traits cause many children to go insane; in others, he said, they cause something perhaps more suspicious: genius.

His argument devolves into being wildly racist, sexist, and anti-Semitic.

Lombroso points out that there are many Jewish geniuses. That said, given his belief that genius is a sign of degeneration, this is a nineteenth-century version of a backhanded compliment. In an anti-Semitic rant, he writes, "It is curious to note that the Jewish elements in the population furnish four and even six times as many lunatics as the rest of the population."

He also argues that women are rarely geniuses. "It is an old observation that while thousands of women apply themselves to music for every hundred men, there has not been a single great woman composer." Rather than acknowledging the lack of opportunity for women, he concludes that women are temperamentally opposed to trying new things. "Women have often stood in the way of progressive movements."

Clearly, Lombroso was no suffragist, and his arguments continue to degenerate. He claimed that insanity and genius are impacted by both the weather and altitude. Countries, he goes on to say, need a hilly region to give rise to a lot of geniuses. "All flat countries—Belgium, Holland, Egypt—are deficient in men of genius."

Why does Lombroso think a hilly, warm climate is instrumental to insanity and genius? Because to him, while insanity is hereditary, it is catalyzed by diseases, such as malaria and leprosy, that flourish in temperate climates.

These and other sensationalist views of genius were popular during the late nineteenth century. John Nisbet's *The Insanity of Genius* came out the same year as Lombroso's book. Both books said that it was the "average man" who was superior, while the genius was overdeveloped in *only* one skill (be it art or science) and thus deficient.

These books were why, at the end of the nineteenth century, genius was viewed by both scientists and the public as an innate, hereditary trait that cannot be fostered or amplified (other than by getting sick). At the same time, genius became tightly and negatively coupled with insanity and madness. Given that, how did we evolve from that view of creativity to the more worshipful view of genius that we hold today?

The IQ of Termites

The transformation of genius from a negative into a positive trait started in Johnson County, Indiana, on the Terman family farm in the late 1800s. The farm was large for the region, having some 640 acres in all. Thanks to the success of the farm, the Terman family could afford the best farm equipment money could buy, as well as an abundance of cows, sheep, chickens, and turkeys.

The elder Terman was a collector. He collected land, animals, books (the Termans had almost two hundred books in their family library), and children (he had fourteen). Of all his offspring, his son Lewis was particularly special to him.

Lewis was ten and the youngest of his sons. He stood out from the others with his shimmering red hair. He also hated sports and outdoor activities. In the evening, you could usually find him holed up, reading.

Armed with a restless curiosity, Lewis had few outlets in Johnson County other than books. So when a salesman came to the door one night hawking a book on phrenology, Lewis was intrigued.

First introduced in Europe in the late 1700s, phrenology was a "science" focusing on the brain's structure and how it affected people's personalities. Phrenologists theorized that certain sections of the brain influenced different traits, and that the size of those sections indicated the strength or the weakness of that trait. Phrenologists claimed to be able to tell whether someone would be a high-achiever, or lazy and unproductive, just by running their hands over that person's skull. While it was often used as a basis for racism, that night it was more like palm reading for the skull.

Lewis was mesmerized by the phrenologist's spiel. That evening, the salesman dazzled the family with stories and demonstrations, going around the room and evaluating the skulls of every single family member, predicting their futures.

When he got to Lewis, the salesman told the young boy that magnificent achievements lay ahead—that he was destined for success.

And without even knowing it, this door-to-door salesman set in motion a series of events that would change how the world understands genius.

Lewis Terman gained two things that evening: self-confidence and a keen interest in personality differences. He began to wonder why some people (like himself) were destined for great things and others were not.

His life seemed to bear out the phrenologist's prophecy. He bounded through school, skipping grades and impressing teachers. While most of his peers were stuck working the fields and tending to livestock, Lewis took a different route. Thanks to the financial support of his parents, he was able to continue his education, attending Indiana University and enrolling in a psychology Ph.D. program at Clark University in Massachusetts. His dissertation topic focused on evaluating the "mental and physical abilities of smart and dull children."

In the early 1900s, society viewed smart children with suspicion or even disdain. This was partially a result of the mad genius literature from the late 1800s. Intelligent people and geniuses were widely regarded as poorly adjusted and fraught with anxieties. Terman believed that testing and study could prove otherwise.

Before long, he had become one of the early researchers in the emerging field of psychology. He landed a job at Stanford University, where his fascination with intelligence only grew. It was here that he heard about the first IQ test, designed by Alfred Binet in France, which was designed to identify students with learning and development disabilities. Terman had a different idea. What if you used the Binet test to assess for genius?

Terman set out to Americanize the content of Binet's test and standardize the scores so that 100 would be the median result. Working with a team at Stanford, he named his version of the test the Stanford-Binet test. Like the phrenologist from his childhood, Terman believed that genius was inherited and could (and, in fact, must) be measured in order to advance humanity. To nurture innate talent, you must first know who had it.

In 1916, believing that everyone should be tested, Terman wrote

The Measurement of Intelligence, a book that included an IQ test that readers could take at home in less than an hour.

The book made Terman an academic celebrity. Yet despite his fame, it took World War I to make IQ testing mainstream, when the U.S. Army agreed to test the IQs of all 1.7 million draftees. For the first time, intelligence testing became accepted in America.

But there was a dark side to Terman's testing. Like many academics of his era, Terman was a believer in eugenics: a practice of trying to "improve" a population through forced sterilizations, abortions, or worse against people a society views as lesser. He wanted to prove that the intelligent were well adjusted, and that society should be mostly concerned with the people who lacked smarts, not those who had it. To that end, he supported the sterilization of the "feebleminded," a desire that tragically became law in some U.S. states like North Carolina, which led to the forced sterilization of some people based on their low IQ test results.

On his quest to prove the superiority of the intelligent, Terman decided that he would track a group of children over the course of their lives. His reasoning was this: How would the lives of students with high IQs unfold? Would they be normal? Successful? Or would the Victorian image of the neurotic, mad genius be true? In 1921, he assembled a group of 1,521 young geniuses through testing and the nomination of their teachers. Those tested had an IQ over 135.

In a somewhat awkward play on Terman's name, these students became known as "Termites." For the rest of their lives (to this day, in fact), they received surveys every five to ten years to assess their progress in life. Terman's hypothesis was that if he was able to identify and track the lives of high-IQ individuals starting at a young age, he would most likely see two distinct things. First, they would be well-adjusted and free of anxiety. Second, they would enjoy tremendous success in their lives.

In fact, the study found something entirely different. While Terman *did* find that geniuses were well-adjusted (their rates of alcoholism, suicide, and divorce fell into the "normal" range), they were surprisingly average, as well, on a different measure: their success.

Yes, a few Termites became prominent, but no one achieved groundbreaking success or won the Nobel Prize or became a household name. In fact, two future Nobel Prize winners were tested by Terman as children and did *not* reach the genius benchmark.

In 1968, after Terman's death, one of his protégés sought to evaluate how the Termites were doing at the halfway point of their professional careers.

She compared the hundred Termites who had achieved the greatest professional success in their careers against the others who had, in her perspective, seemingly stumbled, working at blue-collar jobs like carpentry and as retail clerks. Did the low-achievers have a much lower IQ?

In fact, the difference in IQ between the two groups was immaterial. Where they differed was in those characteristics attributed to nurture. The successful group had more "confidence, persistence and early parental encouragement." Terman's assumptions about intelligence were completely off-base. A high IQ did *not* lead to greater success.

That being said, his successful evangelism on behalf of the IQ test did demonstrate one thing: People with high IQs were normal and well-adjusted. Terman succeeded in helping change the perception of genius to being a positive attribute.

This is a quick version of the path that has led to today's version of the inspiration theory of creativity: the idea that creativity results from a mysterious internal process punctuated by random flashes of inspiration. Today we may still see geniuses often as neurotic (think Steve Jobs or Elon Musk), but they are no longer seen as dangerous, or deserving of castigation. Today, genius is seen as something to be celebrated. But, if Terman's study showed that IQ and creativity are not tied together, where does creative talent come from?

4

What Is Talent?

Name as many uncommon uses for a hair dryer as you can. I'll give you thirty seconds.

Did you come up with half a dozen? More than that? Maybe you thought of blowing dust off surfaces. Or maybe you had a grandparent who taught you that a hair dryer could make cake frosting look glossy.

This type of question is what researchers call a *divergent thinking test*. According to academics, divergent thinking—where the goal is to come up with numerous solutions to problems—is correlated with creativity: the more divergent your thinking, the more creative you are. By looking at the number and originality of your responses, they believe they can accurately assess a person's creative potential.

Researchers in Austria wanted to further understand the relationship between intelligence and creativity. Did you need a high IQ in order to have creative talent? If so, how high?

To investigate, they recruited 297 people to participate in a study. Some were recruited from a university's student population, while others were recruited from the surrounding community.

First, the researchers assessed the IQ of each participant. Then they had them answer six divergent-thinking questions to measure their creative potential. Finally, they had a trained panel evaluate the originality of each answer on a scale of one (not original) to four (very original).

What did the results say?

There are multiple ways to measure creative potential. One is to look at how many ideas people come up with.

What the researchers found was that IQ and the *quantity* of ideas that people came up with were strongly correlated—but only up to an IQ of 86 (below the average IQ of 100). Beyond an IQ of 86, that relationship broke down. Meaning that someone with an IQ of 90—below average—could have just as many ideas as someone with an IQ of 150—a certified "genius."

This is what scientists call the "threshold theory"—the idea that above a certain IQ threshold, every person on earth has the same creative potential.

An IQ threshold of 86 means that roughly the top 80 percent of the population (in terms of IQ score) has the same creative potential. That is a substantial group.

But what if creativity isn't just the *number* of ideas that one comes up with?

The researchers also looked at a more rigorous definition of creative potential: the *quality* of the ideas that individuals came up with.

When they looked at quality, they *again* found an IQ correlation, yet *again* only up to a point. This time the correlation stopped at those people with an IQ of 104.

This means that anyone with an IQ over 104 has the same *potential* to come up with original ideas as someone who falls in the genius IQ range. That, too, is a large group: 40 percent of the population. If you're reading a nonfiction book, like the one in your hands right now, chances are you fall into that group. Worldwide, that is roughly three billion people. Again, that's a huge number of people who share the same creative potential as the genius elite many people idolize.

How can you release that latent potential?

Thirteen Years of Paint

Do you have to be born with precocious talent to be a great artist? Or can you become one through practice and hard work? More generally, is artistic talent innate? This is a key question in the study of creativity.

One seemingly normal man, Jonathan Hardesty, decided to find out.

Hardesty reminds me of the chatty uncle who speaks to everyone at my family reunion. He is bubbly and talkative, with a bronze-colored beard and matching glasses that I suspect are relics of a bygone decade. A familiar face you'd see at a restaurant or say hello to in a bookstore. What he doesn't look like is a classical painter. However, Hardesty's works can fetch five figures. He is not only one of today's most talented fine artists, but also a prolific instructor who teaches virtually all over the world.

His studio, which I saw through the lens of a webcam we used for our video call, is what can best be described as a large shed in his yard. Paintings hang from the walls and lean on every piece of furniture. Hardesty uses the space not only to paint, but to teach through online courses.

Hardesty didn't always want to be a painter. Other than going through a brief artistic phase at the age of eight, he did not pick up a pencil or brush to draw seriously until after college.

In 2002, having recently graduated and gotten married, Hardesty was working as an assistant at the fundraising office for a university medical center, filing papers, helping with donor research, and doing grunt work.

To hear him describe it, it was a cliché of a bureaucratic office environment. "I'd walk in and look around, and people would be scrambling to get to the last sun-dried tomato bagel from the conference room."

His boss was dismissive, and disinterested in him. Hardesty spent countless days filing and organizing papers, only to have to file yet more papers the next day. Eventually, to keep himself sane, he decided to pour himself into his work. If he had to be an assistant, he could at least strive to be the best possible one.

To that end, he tried to figure out if the university he worked for could improve its office procedures. By digitizing its filing process, it could potentially have a huge time-savings opportunity. By taking that on, he could make his life easier *and* save the university some money. But his boss immediately shut him down. The fundraising office was *not* looking for digital transformation.

Looking around the office, Hardesty realized that all his coworkers were miserable. Everyone seemed to loathe their work.

At that point, he realized he had to make a change. "I felt like my soul was dying," Hardesty told me.

He decided to be intentional about his life. He would research the perfect job. What would make him truly happy? He ignored his filing duties and spent the rest of the day scribbling down ideas in a notepad.

Hardesty knew he had to dedicate himself to the next job. His bad habit of bouncing between interests was wearing on him. One month he wanted to be a geologist and emptied the library of its geology books. The next month he'd drop geology and was "committed" to getting a pilot license. For a while, he dreamed of being a musician. Envisioning himself a future rock star, he joined a local Pearl Jam wannabe band. His grunge rock band developed a small measure of fame, but the life of a touring musician was a recipe for boredom, "I didn't like it. It was very monotonous. It was three or four nights a week of the same exact thing."

He brainstormed different career options. What jobs would allow him to be at home, near his wife and, someday, his children? And could he avoid an office environment? He wanted a creative work culture, not one that reminded him of a random DMV.

Hardesty hashed through various options and found a career that fit the bill: a painter! Artists practiced their trade from their homes or their studios, then shipped their work to galleries, where it was sold. As a fine artist, he would be near his wife and future children, far away from pale gray office ceiling tiles. It was perfect.

The only problem was that the last time he had tried painting was back when he was eight. Nor had he grown up in a family where art was emphasized or valued.

Nevertheless, that night he made a pact with himself: He would draw or paint every day until he became a great painter.

Hardesty's first drawing was a self-portrait. He was proud when the work was completed, but also horrified. The character looked more like the fictional oddball Napoleon Dynamite than it did Hardesty. Yet while the self-portrait was mediocre, he had fun creating it.

To get honest feedback, he started a thread on ConceptArt.org, a message board for artists. The post was titled *Journey of an Absolute Rookie: Paintings and Sketches*, and in it he wrote, "I am starting from rock bottom and I am going to paint at least one painting and do at least one sketch every day . . . probably two on the weekends. The order you see them in is the order that I am painting and/or sketching them . . . every day starting on 9/15/02. I am baring my soul to everyone. I will post everything I do . . . whether it is awful or not."

Hardesty hoped he would gather helpful feedback. For those interested in creativity, however, his postings are also an extraordinary record of one person's attempt to learn a new skill. For the next thirteen years, he posted continuously on his thread, updating his followers with his progress and uploading his latest paintings. Below you can see one of his very first drawings from 2002, alongside a painting from five years later.

Jonathan Hardesty painting scans. Copyright © 2002 and 2007. Reprinted with permission of Jonathan Hardesty.

Needless to say, Hardesty had improved tremendously over the years. But how? Lots of people paint as a hobby, even for decades, but few reach his level of skill and accomplishment.

So how had he gotten so good?

Becoming an Expert

How do you learn to master a new skill?

Most people would say, "Practice, practice, practice." You may even have heard the (as we'll discuss) faulty notion of the "10,000-hour rule."

However, neither of these ideas gives us a satisfactory answer. Many people practice a skill for a long time but come nowhere near the level of world-class expertise. Think about driving. Most of us have spent thousands of hours behind the wheel, yet few if any of us are professional NASCAR drivers. In fact, studies show that years of experience often bear little relationship with skill.

One study looked at experienced stock pickers and found that on average, they were no better at investing than novices. Another study found that experienced therapists do not have better patient outcomes than new therapists.

It turns out that it is *not* simply years one spends on *doing*—that is, experience—that is tied to success. There is something else at work.

Researchers who study expertise decided to look at the problem in a different way. What if you compared high performers to lower performers in a specific skill? What differences might you find in how the two groups trained and learned?

One researcher compared elite sprinters to merely decent sprinters. They found that there was not only a physical difference between the two, but also a *mental* one.

Elite sprinters focus on "monitoring their internal states more closely and focus more on planning their race performance during competition than less accomplished runners."

Another study evaluated elite chess players and reached a similar conclusion: expert players had more advanced mental patterns of critical chess positions, allowing them to play better than average players.

These patterns are what psychologists call "mental models," your brain's representations of concepts or situations. For example, your concept of what a negotiation is like (two sides, going back and forth, trying to find a solution) would be a mental model.

Researchers found the importance of mental models across all types of skills. Additional studies have found similar patterns of enhanced mental models in medical professionals, computer programmers, and video game players.

So how do you learn these mental models if it is not simple experience?

This is where many people fall back on a comfortable answer: talent. They'll tell you some people are born with certain skills. It is nature, not nurture. Rather than try, they kick back and decide to watch *America's Got Talent*, believing that the eight-year-old who can breathe fire simply was born with "it."

To explore the talent question, researchers decided to see if they could train normal people to accomplish superhuman things.

For example, look at the string of digits below. Memorize as many digits as you can. Take your time, there is no rush.

3895850258250259050150185100994445151051058119581509819508109581059810958109581293567

When you think you've memorized as many as you can, look away from the digits and try to recall them.

The sequence above has 80 digits. How many did you remember? Four? Ten? None?

I usually get about six. Researchers found that the typical college student usually remembers seven (making me feel bad for my lowly six). If you got more than that, give yourself a pat on the back.

Here's where researchers found something surprising, even seemingly impossible. If they trained average college students using well-known memorization techniques, the students were ultimately able to surpass *80 digits*. This study has been repeated multiple times. One researcher summarized the study of these memorization skills by saying, "Recent reviews have not found any scientifically verified evidence that would limit motivated healthy adults, with appropriate instruction and training, from acquiring exceptional levels of performance for specific types of memory tasks."

It wasn't hereditary talent that dramatically improved the memory skills of the students—it also wasn't 10,000 hours of practice (an often repeated but incorrect number that we will discuss later). No, it was the *way* in which they were trained.

One study that looked at highly skilled artists found that roughly half were child prodigies, while the other half had "undistinguished childhoods, and were not recognized as exceptional until early adulthood." Perhaps we don't have to be geniuses to excel in creative fields. We just have to train like them.

South Dakota: An Artist's Paradise

Jonathan Hardesty's path to becoming a master painter took him to an unconventional place: South Dakota.

Hardesty was getting lots of online encouragement. Someone with the username Gekitsu—who possessed excellent grammar—said, "i feel he won't stop practising until he ownz us all i wish i had that energy."

For his part, Hardesty was drawing or painting every day, and though he initially made quick strides, Hardesty's progress stalled. Self-doubt started to seep into his forum posts. In May of 2003, he posted online, "I am so frustrated at my lack of ability . . . I feel like quitting . . . don't worry I won't . . . but I definitely feel like it tonight . . . I can't visualize anything in 3d . . . I can't control a pencil or a pen . . . bleh . . . I'm going to bed."

He needed a new way to learn, but how?

Online, he stumbled across a training movement called the atelier movement. This training has origins from the pre-Renaissance era when artists were viewed as craftsmen and learned their art in workshops. In that time, master painters took on a handful of apprentices in their studios who were trained to perfectly replicate the master's work.

This model became less dominant during the Italian Renaissance, as wealthy patrons began funding individual artists and elite academies. However, in the 1800s a French artist named Jean-Léon Gérôme brought back the workshop (or *atelier* in French) model and started training students in his studio. He taught numerous painters, many of whom went on to have successful careers.

The modern version of atelier involves four years of full-time study. Throughout, students spend hours each day drawing hyperrealistic sketches of sculptures, a set of classic drawings (called "Bargue drawings"), and live models. Eventually, they add in black and white paint. Only in their final year do they start practicing the essentials of color. After four years, students will have spent thousands of hours slowly perfecting the fundamentals of painting.

The more Hardesty read about this model, the more interested he became. He was convinced this program would teach him the essentials of great painting. He buzzed around the Web, reading all he could on the various ateliers in the United States. Finally, he found one that seemed ideal. It had a respected teacher and an open spot. There was one problem: It was in Sioux Falls, South Dakota.

He asked his wife if she would be willing to move there. She said yes, but her family was skeptical. They were worried that their son-in-law was going on a wild-goose chase. They weren't the only ones, either. A contingent of posters on his thread thought it was a scam and warned him to stay away.

Nonetheless, Hardesty packed up his life, and he and his wife drove to South Dakota.

His initial excitement soon faded in the face of the harsh realities of life as an unpaid artist in South Dakota. He got a job at Breadsmith, a local bakery, where he worked for eight hours every morning, starting at 5:00 a.m.. After work each day, he went to the atelier, painted until 9:00 p.m., slept, and repeated it all the next day.

They weren't just short on time, they were also short on money. Sometimes when bills came in, Hardesty and his wife would face a cash crunch. Hardesty remembers one time when they had only a few dollars left.

They were at a local grocery store shopping for the cheapest food possible. Sick of cheap carbs, they were in search of something with protein. Scurrying around the supermarket, they stumbled upon a bag of lentils. Full of protein, it was also inexpensive—39 cents a bag; the perfect food for a struggling couple.

For the next three weeks, they survived on lentils and bread until they saved some money. Hardesty, having consumed a lifetime's worth of lentils, won't touch them to this day.

Nevertheless this scrappy time in South Dakota was what crystalized his transformation.

What was it about this training regimen that changed Hardesty?

Being Purposeful

You might have heard of the "10,000-hour rule." Malcom Gladwell coined it in his 2008 bestselling book *Outliers*. Since the book's publication, the idea that with 10,000 hours of practice anyone can become an expert has become a mantra in business and self-improvement circles. According to Google, now over 140,000 websites reference the phrase.

The rule comes from research by K. Anders Ericsson, a Swedish-born professor at Florida State University, who is a grandfather of the research on developing skill. However, according to Ericsson, there is a problem: The rule is not strictly accurate, or, as he put it to me, "Gladwell misread our paper."

There are two main flaws with the 10,000-hour rule. First, it neglects to mention that it's not simply how many hours you spend that's important, but *how* you spend those hours. As I mentioned earlier, highly experienced therapists and stock pickers don't necessarily get better results than novices.

The reason why is that most people, once they achieve an adequate degree of skill, stop trying to consciously improve. Think about driving. On your commute, you are not trying to get better at turning or accelerating. You are comfortable with your current level of skill. When you first started driving, you were—I hope—aware of every aspect of handling a car: how to turn properly, how to slow down and not rear-end the vehicle in front of you, how to parallel park (a maneuver I still avoid). As you worked on these skills, you slowly got better and better, probably without realizing it. However, over time, these skills became ingrained and subconscious. Driving became an automatic activity.

The result is that as you continued driving for thousands of hours, you did *not* go on to learn more advanced skills. If you believe the 10,000-hour rule, every person with a driver's license should eventually develop the skills of a race-car driver. My guess is, however, that although you've probably spent 10,000 hours driving, you are still a typical driver. Ericsson explained why. "Automaticity is the enemy of growing your expertise," he said. "If you end up automating things, then you lose that ability to actually control what you're doing." If you can't control it, you can't improve it.

Instead of simply practicing a task over and over again for 10,000 hours, Ericsson's research shows you have to engage extensively in *purposeful practice*. This is a particular type of practice where you work on one small skill repeatedly, with a clear goal and a feedback mechanism. Think about practicing your parallel parking with a driving instructor. Usually, the feedback comes from a teacher or experienced mentor. As you master the small skills, you advance to more difficult ones.

Ericsson carried out a study where he examined expert violinists to demonstrate the power of purposeful practice. What he found was that all the violinists spent roughly the same amount of time practicing per week, but the best violinists spent more of those hours engaged in *purposeful* practice. Ten thousand hours alone *did not* lead to better performance. Ericsson gave me an example of how the violin students would engage in this more effective practice. A teacher would listen to a student's performance and pick out flaws. Maybe they were playing too quickly. Maybe they were too slow. The teacher would then assign exercises that specifically focused on playing tempos correctly. The student would practice these exercises over and over again, and only once the teacher agreed that they had mastered them would they move on to more difficult skills.

This approach doesn't just work for music. Research found similar results among chess players: The number of hours of purposeful practice was "the best predictor of chess skill"—not the number of games played.

Non-purposeful practice, which is practicing things you already know how to do, just reinforces mental processes that are already established. Purposeful practice allows the student to gain new mental methods and thereby improve their abilities.

The second serious flaw with the 10,000-hour rule is that Ericsson's study did *not* find that 10,000 hours of even *purposeful* practice would make you an expert. Instead, it found that 10,000 hours of purposeful practice was the *average* of the experts he studied. Some achieved it with significantly fewer hours, others achieved it with more. As Ericsson explained to me, "This idea that the body or the cells in your body would keep track of how many hours of practice you engaged in, and that there's some magical clock at 10,000 hours that changes things is a curious belief."

Instead, Ericsson believes that the number of hours someone needs to master a task is different for different people, and for different tasks. For example, to master skills that have fewer people pursuing them, becoming an expert should require less time. Remember the digit memorization study? Unlike the violin or chess, there are far fewer people trying to become world class digit memorizers, so when researchers trained people, Ericsson told me, "They were able to basically become the best in the world in about four hundred hours." That is only 4 percent of the 10,000-hour rule. When Ericcson first studied digit memorization, you could have become the world champion, memorizing more than 80 digits, in a year's worth of weekend practice. Things change, and today the current record for digit span requires that you memorize over 450 digits—a feat that would take considerably longer to achieve.

On the other hand, in some popular fields, it can take much *more* than 10,000 hours. Ericsson explained to me that when you look at people who win international piano competitions, they typically spend around 25,000 hours before attaining that level of performance.

In short, mastering a skill takes many, many hours of purposeful practice and the specific number of hours varies. Unfortunately, the phenomenon of mastering a skill is hard to study since most experts do not bother to keep records of their practice regimen.

Without knowing it, Jonathan Hardesty had stumbled into becoming one of the few documented, public examples of someone engaging in extensive purposeful practice. In an atelier, students spend roughly 6,000 hours of purposeful practice over a four-year period. Overall, Hardesty estimates that between his formal and informal training, he has put in well over 25,000 hours of purposeful practice. Consequently, he has gone from drawing self-portraits that look like Napoleon Dynamite to creating paintings that would make any art student drip with envy.

Hardesty continues this form of purposeful practice to this day. Even though he is now a master painter, he is *still* trying to improve. He explained, "I still have lots of flaws in my work. I'm working just as hard as when I was first learning."

He is currently working on "brush efficiency," where a painter works to create an effect with as few strokes as possible by carefully controlling the pressure of the brush on the canvas. To improve on this aspect of his work, Hardesty developed a method of purposeful practice. He explained, "At the end of each session when I have leftover paint, I'll do a stroke on a scrap piece of canvas. Then I'll try to duplicate that stroke exactly. I'll try to duplicate the randomness of that stroke. That requires the right amount of paint, the right pressure application. It's like a doctor with surgery."

Today, Hardesty has launched his own online atelier, called Classical Art Online, to offer this method of teaching to people who can't afford to move to South Dakota for four years, or don't want to.

He is also applying his love of learning to a new skill. Hardesty now spends his free time in a different kind of studio: a jujitsu gym.

In fact, Hardesty has become a lover of the learning process, "It's really fun to be on the bottom of the totem pole again in something."

His new goal? To compete in an MMA fight before his knees give out.

Once again, he has some doubters. As Hardesty tells me with a smile, "My wife still laughs. Now she's like, 'You're not fighting.' And I'm like, 'Okay, love.'"

As we wrap up our interview, he mentions that he's soon going to compete in his first intramural fight. I have no doubt he'll be in an MMA ring soon enough.

Made of Plastic

The question remains: Why does purposeful practice work? To answer this, I went to a surprising source: taxi drivers.

Saul was a London cabbie. He drove one of those famous black taxis with hunchbacked roofs (this was pre-Uber). He spent his days driving the streets of London, taking customers to their desired destinations. Some destinations were requested over and over, such as the airport, while others were places he'd never been before, such as an obscure neighborhood where a customer's mother lived. As a result, Saul, like most London cab drivers, developed a keen ability to navigate.

One day Saul saw a newspaper advertisement inviting taxi drivers to participate in a neurological research study. He called the phone number.

Soon Saul was in the offices of researchers at University College London. They were planning to scan the brains of taxi drivers to see whether years of driving a cab might cause measurable changes in a driver's brain.

Along with eighteen other London taxi drivers, Saul agreed to participate in the study and was put through a battery of tests. He answered questions about his beliefs, values, and personal history.

An MRI machine allows the researchers to observe the structure of someone's brain. When the researchers conducted MRI scans of the taxi drivers' brains, they found something unexpected. The rear hippocampus of their brains tended to be enlarged. This is the area of the brain that is critical for understanding where we are spatially and how to navigate. It is activated, for example, when we use landmarks such as a large tree or a memorial to figure out how to get home.

In short, the taxi drivers' brains were structured to make it easier for them to get around London.

That leads to the obvious question: Was Saul's brain naturally organized that way, thereby influencing his decision to join the taxi driver profession? Or did being a taxi driver somehow alter Saul's brain structure?

To answer this, the researchers compared the brains of taxi drivers to those of another group of professionals who spent their days driving around London: bus drivers.

What they found, when controlling for other variables, was that bus drivers did *not* show the same increase in the size of the hippocampus. Why? Because bus drivers follow the same route day after day, whereas taxi drivers are regularly tasked with making their way to different, and sometimes unfamiliar, destinations. To put it simply, taxi drivers engage in a form of purposeful practice related to navigation. Customers give them instructions, they have to figure out how to get to this and that destination (this was before GPS), and then they receive either positive or negative feedback depending on how well or poorly they did.

Over time, it seems, this purposeful practice actually changes the structure of taxi drivers' brains.

A second piece of evidence supported this same conclusion. Tests on taxi drivers with different numbers of years on the job revealed that the rear hippocampus increased depending on how many years a cabbie had been driving. The more experience a cabbie had navigating the streets of London, the larger their hippocampus.

Similar correlations have been found with other skills. Studies have shown that musicians, bilingual speakers, and even jugglers experience changes in their brain structure over time as they practice and learn more.

This concept, that our brains' physiology adapts to situations and experiences, is known as *brain plasticity*.

In fact, even short training experiences have been shown to affect brain structure. One study found that training sessions as simple as a short vocabulary lesson affect it. Another study found that ten 60-minute computer-training sessions for elderly people had a measurable effect on brain performance that persisted *ten years later.*

How, though?

To find out, I spoke to Joyce Shaffer, a scientist at the University of Washington and an expert in brain plasticity. She believes that an underlying mechanism is neurogenesis, the continuous generation of new brain cells. According to one study, both men and women create over 1,400 new brain cells every day.

Once new brain cells are created, they take eight weeks to mature. During that time, they migrate to the most active areas of your brain. If you are a cabbie, constantly navigating London, these new brain cells join forces with the part of your brain that controls your navigation skills. As a result, your brain starts to adapt to the skills you are learning. As Shaffer describes it, "You can influence the career choice of that brain cell."

Furthermore, if you don't challenge these cells with new experiences, they risk dying off.

Put another way, *learning* causes our brains to retain new brain cells. These new cells connect with the specific parts of your brain that are being activated. According to Shaffer, "We totally underestimate how much we can modify our brains for improved chemistry, architecture, and performance."

When researchers control for other variables, they often find that people who are experts in a particular field did *not* demonstrate any special abilities early on in their lives. Instead, one of two things happened. First, a child may have learned a skill from another activity. For example, if you taught your five-year-old son how to play softball, by the time he is seven, he will have more experience running, and a parent may easily mistake that as a natural talent for running track.

Second, it is natural for most parents to tell a child that they are particularly good at something, even if the child is merely average. This leads to a positive feedback loop in which the child invests more time in practicing that skill, thereby garnering ever-increasing amounts of positive feedback. Over many years that can compound into exceptional ability.

Another study demonstrated that when you dig into their backgrounds, "elite athletes and other expert performers had different developmental histories compared to their peers. The elite performers started early with supervised training and gained access to some of the best teachers and training environments."

In short, research shows that exceptional talent is not always the result of winning the genetic lottery, but instead the outcome of immense amounts of structured, purposeful practice. While the notion of giftedness stems from Lewis Terman's popularization of IQ tests, research since then reveals that people of all backgrounds have more creative potential than they realize, and that IQ is not correlated with creative potential for people of average or higher intelligence.

If science shows us that creative "genius" is a learned skill, and purposeful practice allows us to radically enhance our skills, can we engage in purposeful practice to become more creative?

The answer is yes. But to understand how, it is important to understand first how society decides that something is "creative" or that someone is a "genius."

What Is a Genius?

C harles Darwin was panicked. The now elderly, wealthy naturalist reread the letter he'd gotten from a younger scientist, Alfred Wallace, a man he knew came from a humble background with only six years of formal education in a one-room schoolhouse in Hertfordshire, a largely agricultural city in southern England.

Darwin himself began his scientific career at age twenty-two as a "gentleman naturalist." His father was a doctor, and one of his grandfathers had written *Zoonomia*, an early book in the field of biology. His family was well-off and educated. Darwin subsequently earned a university degree, benefiting from exposure to more progressive intellectuals, many of whom questioned the rigid scientific norms of the nineteenth century.

But as we shall see, Wallace held the upper hand in this moment.

After college, one of Darwin's professors recommended young Charles for a position as an onboard naturalist for the HMS *Beagle* as it voyaged to South America. Hungry for adventure, Darwin applied for and got the job.

For the next five years, he traveled the world on the *Beagle*. He spent much of that time trying to maintain a detailed diary. His periods on the ocean were punctuated by weeks or months on land, exploring the beautiful South American wilds.

During the voyage, Darwin found himself visiting the Galapagos Islands. Seeing the differences among mockingbirds, he realized that the birds differed based on the particular island they inhabited. Legend has it that Darwin had an epiphany in thinking about the birds, and the theory of natural selection came to him in a light-bulb moment! At least that was the story I was taught in my eighth-grade science class, along with many generations of middle-school students.

In truth, however, Darwin simply noticed that there were mockingbirds with different features. His response was mere surprise. There was no light-bulb moment as to why the differences existed. No dramatic revelations occurred. His development of the natural selection concept wouldn't take place for several more years.

Returning to England, Darwin labored to turn his ship diary into a book, *The Voyage of the Beagle*. It was published in 1839 and made Darwin a celebrity scientist, a nineteenth-century Neil deGrasse Tyson. The book sparked a frenzy of interest around the specimens Darwin collected. He regaled audiences with the stories of his adventures, and his celebrity continued to increase.

It wasn't until 1842 that Darwin began to put together his theory of natural selection. He had been reflecting on his specimens for years and had finally come to his revolutionary conclusion. There was only one problem. By that point, Darwin was a highly regarded member of the scientific establishment. He was a member of both the Athenaeum Club, a coveted private association, and the Royal Society, the elite scientific association of his era. Despite his own rebellious nature, he nonetheless enjoyed the fame and fortune that accompanied his scientific standing. And he knew that if he publicized his latest theory, he would be labeled a heretic or, worse, ostracized from society. At the time, science was subservient to God. Evolution would mean that God hadn't made Earth's creatures in a sudden flash.

Darwin kept quiet about his theory, though over the years he discreetly told a few friends about it. In the 1850s, his friends encouraged Darwin to publicize his theory. In response, Darwin started to write his book. In poor health and in self-imposed exile at his country house, Darwin spent his time and sparse energy writing.

On June 18, 1858, the nine-page letter from Alfred Wallace showed up in the mail.

Wallace's first career was as a surveyor, where he learned how to note and record details. Finding himself unemployed in 1848, he made the decision to travel to Brazil as an unpaid naturalist.

Upon his return, Wallace published his findings and gained a small following in scientific circles. This minor fame allowed Wallace to obtain funding for a longer, bigger expedition: eight years traveling through the islands of the Philippines and Indonesia.

On this trip, he concluded that the population explosions of certain species could eventually lead to overcrowding and the survival of the fittest—the foundation of natural selection. The concept excited him, but he knew he needed feedback from other scientists, too.

Wallace knew Darwin professionally. Over the years they had corresponded, and Wallace had gone so far as to send Darwin a few of his specimens. He decided to put his ideas on the origin of species to Darwin in a letter. As Darwin was far better known, Wallace felt that Darwin might offer valuable perspective.

When the letter showed up in Darwin's mailbox, the older scientist had already written 250,000 words of his book on natural selection. The book still wasn't complete; he wanted it to be so evidence-rich that no one could deny its argument. But when

Darwin opened Wallace's letter, he knew immediately that his great discovery was in peril. Concerned about his reputation but not wishing to violate the gentlemanly norms of the Victorian era, he sent his work and Wallace's letter to his prominent scientist friends, asking what he should do.

They came up with a "compromise": they would present a paper on natural selection that combined both Darwin's and Wallace's ideas at the Linnean Society, a prominent scientific association. There was one problem: Wallace never agreed to this "compromise." He was somewhere out in the Pacific Ocean and couldn't be reached.

Darwin and Wallace had experienced what academics term "simultaneous invention," a state of affairs where two or more individuals independently come to the very same discovery or conclusion. History is peppered with examples of simultaneous invention. Joseph Swan and Thomas Edison both received American patents for the incandescent light bulb in 1880. And Elisha Gray and Alexander Graham Bell both patented the telephone on the same exact day: March 7, 1876.

In the case of natural selection, the story is even more complicated. Not only did Wallace discover it at the same time Darwin did, but ancient Greek philosophers described something similar thousands of years earlier. Born in 99 BC, Lucretius, a poet and philosopher who, legend has it, died from the side effects of a supposed "love potion," wrote a collection of poems in which he describes the survival of the fittest, a critical element of natural selection:

> And in the ages after monsters died,
> *Perforce there perished many a stock, unable*
> *By propagation to forge a progeny.*
> *For whatsoever creatures thou beholdest*
> *Breathing the breath of life, the same have been*

Even from their earliest age preserved alive
By cunning, or by valour, or at least
By speed of foot or wing. And many a stock
Remaineth yet, because of use to man . . .

All this is to say that nearly two thousand years before Darwin and Wallace, the Greeks had come up with a rudimentary theory of natural selection, as Darwin even acknowledges in the introduction to his book. "But it is very far from true that the principle is a modern discovery. I could give several references to works of high antiquity, in which the full importance of the principle is acknowledged . . . Explicit rules are laid down by some of the Roman classical writers."

History is full of simultaneous inventions. Yet as is often the case, only one of the creators of natural selection is remembered as a genius.

Constructing Genius

When Darwin died, he was given a state funeral and buried in Westminster Abbey. When Alfred Wallace died, his life was commemorated with a small plaque, also in the Abbey. While they both discovered the theory of natural selection, Wallace is mostly forgotten. The British Natural History Museum recently struggled to raise money for a statue of Alfred Wallace, whereas Darwin is on every schoolchild's lips. What did Darwin do to garner recognition as a genius?

Part of the answer rests in what Wallace *didn't* do. As Darwin was racing to finish his book, Wallace continued to explore islands. Darwin published his opus in 1859, three years before Wallace came back from sea. The book captured the attention of the masses and began to solidify Darwin's reputation.

When Wallace returned, he focused much of his time and

energy on progressive politics. He was an active feminist and also evangelized against eugenics. Unfortunately, this made him lose stature among the scientific establishment, and some scientists treated him as an outsider.

What's more, Wallace deferred to Darwin in a way that seems absurd in retrospect. In writing his own book about natural selection, Wallace went so far as to title his book after his rival (*Darwinism: An Exposition of the Theory of Natural Selection with Some of Its Applications*). One Darwin historian later explained in an interview, "He felt glad to be accepted as a partner, albeit a junior partner, in this great discovery. It seems to be more than he would have hoped for and he was very glad to settle for it."

That said, the story of Darwin and Wallace illustrates a critical point in our understanding of creativity. Genius is, perhaps surprisingly, far from an objective label. For someone to be considered a creative genius, their innovation has to be accepted by the masses. A novelist who writes a riveting book but can't get it published is not remembered by history. The modest scientist who doesn't publicize himself or herself is soon forgotten.

The truth is that when people talk about creativity, they are usually talking about a creative output that is widely adopted or accepted (think Steve Jobs or Pablo Picasso). Of course, this is different from the ability to come up with novel ideas.

Put slightly differently, a person's work has to be accepted by other people to garner the *creative* label, and by even larger numbers of people for a person to be labeled a *creative genius*.

Creative genius, it turns out, is a social phenomenon rather than simply a reflection of how innovative, forward-thinking, or influential any one person is.

WHAT IS A GENIUS?

On a Hill

*As a teenager I lived on the Gianicolo Hill in Rome, overlooking Mi-
chelangelo's great dome. During this time, my father, a redoubtable
amateur art historian, made sure to point out to me the flowering of
Renaissance creativity that surrounded us, I believed him, but I must
confess that those masterpieces by and large made no impression on
me. Some of them did produce an uncanny sense of serenity; others
conveyed a great sense of power, or an undefinable excitement. But
creativity? The great breakthroughs of Western art all looked equally
old and decrepit to me; to think of them as innovations seemed a silly
convention.*

The words above echo something that perhaps we have all felt
at one point—and maybe still do. Maybe as a kid you were dragged
to an art museum by your parents, or as part of an ambitious field
trip in middle school. You stood in front of a painting, confused.
Why is this in a museum? It doesn't seem remarkable. Or perhaps
you saw a work of abstract art and thought to yourself, "I can do
that."

The author of the above passage is Professor Mihaly Csikszentmihalyi. He is known for his bestselling book *Flow*, which popular-
ized the notion of "getting into the flow," and for his TED Talk on
the topic, which has over four million views to date. For students
of creative history, he also provides one of the most complete explanations for how things get labeled as "creative."

Csikszentmihalyi looks like a weathered Santa Claus who ex-
udes not jolliness but a reassuring, Zen-like quality. In fact, he
could be Santa Claus's professorial cousin. In my interview with
him, he explained to me the critical elements of the social phenomenon of creativity.

Creativity is surprisingly hard to identify, he writes, and gives
an example: "An unusual African mask might seem the product

of creative genius, until we realize that the same mask has been carved exactly the same way for centuries."

How does something get labeled as creative? Csikszentmihalyi says three elements come together to generate this label.

Element One: Subject Matter

First, there is what Csikszentmihalyi calls the "domain," or what I call subject matter. In most if not all mediums, these are the norms, practices, and previous creative outputs that are regarded as standards. For example, if we are talking about Catholicism, Csikszentmihalyi told me that the subject matter would include "the New Testament, the Old Testament, and the major contributions of the fathers of the church." It also includes the "responsibilities that a Catholic, a Christian, would have to follow in order to be saved."

Or consider the composition of classical music. Here, the subject matter includes the musical notes themselves, examples of past successful symphonies, and the standards of composition. Any "creative" classical composer needs to be familiar with all of these. To create something novel, you must know what already exists.

Obviously, this presents an obstacle for people who seek acknowledgment as creative individuals. First, they have to learn the standards and the norms of their craft. (I'll explain how they can do this in future chapters.) Second, their work has to somehow become part of this formal subject matter. If you're a painter, for example, you must get into prestigious galleries, museums, and textbooks. Otherwise, your work is far less likely to be considered creative; it will be seen as merely new and/or experimental.

Timing is also essential. Two paintings created in two different eras could yield wildly different results. If Andy Warhol had painted his pop art in the Italian Renaissance, he likely would've been labeled a heretic. If Leonardo da Vinci had painted a classical work during the time of pop art, he would've been seen as creating dated, yet technically precise, art—interesting, but hardly "creative" or revolutionary. That artistic ground had already been broken hundreds of years earlier. Timing is essential to getting your work, and you, labeled *creative*. In the following chapters, I will explain how you can learn to leverage the timing of trends to your advantage.

A thorough understanding of the subject matter allows anyone to understand the familiar baseline of their medium. But how do you get your work to become *part* of the subject matter?

Element Two: Gatekeepers

Csikszentmihalyi calls those who decide what constitutes the subject matter of a type of creativity the "field." I use the term *gatekeepers*. These gatekeepers are responsible for deciding what is creative and has value, and what doesn't. In art, the gatekeepers include gallery owners, art critics, and museum curators. In pop music, they are the managers, producers, and record label executives. For restaurants, it is the reviewer, other chefs, and nowadays, thanks to applications like Yelp, consumers.

If you are a painter who never commands the attention of a gatekeeper, unfortunately you are just another aspiring wannabe, not a creative genius. For better or for worse, the gatekeepers decide what has value, and what will be labeled creative.

For this reason, gatekeepers are a notorious challenge for creative people. Csikszentmihalyi explained to me that often an industry gatekeeper doesn't want to "creatively christen" anyone new. In the world of start-ups, for example, venture capitalists may decide that there are too many Uber or Lyft clones already, and decline to fund a new ride-sharing service. Even if a fledgling company has the potential to become a strong competitor of Uber, it may not be possible to raise the necessary capital to compete.

If you cannot attract the attention of the gatekeepers, you might very well be "original" and "technically skilled," but the truth of the matter is you will not be considered creative. As Csikszentmi-halyi points out, in ancient times a painter's standing was subject to the whims of kings and popes. Today, the group that comprises gatekeepers can be much larger, as the Internet has created a more democratic, less stringent set of gatekeepers. For example, consider the world of romance novels.

Kristen Ashley is one of the queens of self-publishing. She has published fifty-seven books to date, selling over two and a half million copies. She is one of the most prolific romance novelists in the world, and is the poster child for how e-books have transformed the genre.

The romance novel has traditionally had its own set of gatekeepers—traditional book publishers—that prevented certain books from ever seeing the light of day. Inevitably, this slowed the pace of new voices and subjects. However, in 2007, Amazon launched Kindle Direct Publishing. This program made it easier for authors to self-publish, and what's more, Amazon would give them a 70 percent royalty on every copy sold.

Almost overnight, the entire romance genre changed. Now any author could get virtual distribution. By 2013, 61 percent of romance book sales were from e-books. The market had turned digital.

This meant that authors like Kristen Ashley, many of whom had been snubbed by the traditional gatekeepers of publishing, could finally get their voices heard. Very suddenly, new subgenres in the romance category began bubbling up—for example, queer, lesbian, and trans romance. As Kristen Ashley explained to me, "With the independent publishing rage right now, these people are also telling their own stories. There's a lot of empowerment of women going on with these books."

While the Internet has changed the forms of gatekeepers, there is an essential ingredient for fostering creativity: prosperity. Consumers cannot spend time attending art galleries or buying books or records if they do not have discretionary time and income. Universities and research teams need to win grants to conduct new research. Musicians need audiences that are willing to pay for music and concerts. A country's material wealth, and the economic confidence of its natives, is an unspoken enabler of creativity.

So, creativity blossoms whenever the economy grows. The Italian Renaissance was as much a golden age of the Italian economy as it was a golden era of art, as well-heeled families such as the Medici rose to power. It wasn't just royalty and the Church that could afford to commission new art. Now traders and merchants found themselves with money to spend.

Element Three: Individual

The third essential element of creativity is the *individual*. While most of the literature on creativity focuses on the individual, no one exists in a vacuum. No matter what they do, creators first need to live in a place where the economy supports their efforts. Next, they need to know how to create projects that fit the zeitgeist. It perhaps goes without saying that they also need to create something that is technically proficient. Finally, they must successfully reach and persuade the gatekeepers of their profession to christen them as creative.

According to Csikszentmihalyi, not only do individuals need to be technically talented, but they also require a set of practical attributes that allow them to engage with the media, consumers, and gatekeepers. Part of being a successful artist is being a persuasive salesperson for your own brand. You must be able to generate and capture attention. This goes against the notion of the reclusive, angry artist.

Csikszentmihalyi conducted a famous study where he tested and interviewed art students, then tracked their careers over the next few years. What he found was that in school, the students who were the most highly regarded were also the ones who matched the accepted stereotype of the irreverent, neurotic genius. But in the real world of art, these students, unable to sell themselves or their wares, floundered.

Notes Csikszentmihalyi, "The young artists who left their mark on the world of art tended to be those who in addition to originality also had the ability to communicate their vision to the public, often resorting to public relations tactics that would have been abhorrent in the pure atmosphere of the art school."

Personal resources can also play a large unseen role in one's success. If you have access to private education, you will have a far greater chance of getting into a great university with access to future gatekeepers. If your family has money to pay for violin lessons, there is a much higher likelihood that you can become a world-class violin player. Early lessons could give you years to develop an interest and skill, as well as an advantage over other students, which would only compound over time.

The individual also has to be accepted within the system. If you are an outsider, or are marginalized in some way, it is traditionally more difficult to gain access to gatekeepers. Csikszentmihalyi found that during their school years women and men had the same degree of creative potential. But twenty years later when he followed up on his original study, not one of the women had become well known, whereas numerous male study subjects had gained both stature and celebrity. As Csikszentmihalyi wrote, "Until quite recently the majority of scientific advances were made by men who had the means and the leisure—clergymen like Copernicus, tax collectors like Lavoisier, or physicians like Galvani—men who could afford to build their own laboratories and concentrate on their thoughts."

The result is that when you study the history of creative geniuses, you find people who had the opportunity to learn the right skills, the time to master those skills, and the ability to persuade others that their work had value. This helps pave the way for the gatekeepers to accept the work of these aspiring geniuses, and add it to the established subject matter or canon, which the mainstream population then looks to as the definition of what should be deemed creative.

All these elements—the subject matter, the gatekeepers, and the individual—have to align for an individual or a work to merit the label "creative." Csikszentmihalyi summed it up in his writing: "Originality, freshness of perceptions, divergent thinking ability are all well and good in their own right, as desirable personal traits. But without some form of public recognition they do not constitute creativity, and certainly not genius."

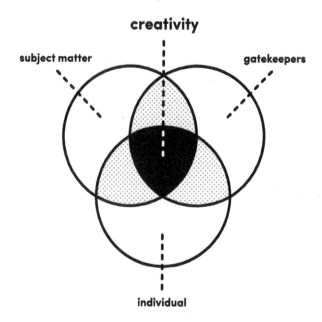

This is all a roundabout way of reminding us that creativity and genius are *social phenomena*. As we've learned, with the right training most people can learn the technical skills that are needed to create high-quality work as Jonathan Hardesty did. Yet training alone will not make a person's work "creative" and will not admit them to the pantheon of artists. People must also receive public recognition—and crucial to that recognition is *timing*. You need to be producing or creating work at the moment when both resources exist and gatekeepers are interested. So in addition to honing your salesmanship skills and maneuvering yourself into an environment that supports your creative field, you need to have the right idea at the right time.

If Paul McCartney had written "Yesterday" in 1885, one has to wonder whether anyone would have cared. "Yesterday" would have come across as too different. If J. K. Rowling had written Harry Potter in 1650, no one would have read it and she may have been burned at the stake!

If timing is essential, can we learn how to master that? Is there a way to engage in purposeful practice to improve our timing?

Surprisingly, the answer is yes.

The Creative Curve

Think of the most famous person you know of named Lisa.

Who did you think of?

Lisa Marie Presley? Lisa Kudrow from *Friends*? Lisa Bonet from *The Cosby Show*? Maybe the comedian Lisa Lampanelli?

I've asked this question to audiences ranging from teenagers to Fortune 500 executives, and I usually get one of the above answers. (Lisa from *The Simpsons* doesn't count.)

All the Lisas I mentioned share one trait: they were born in the 1960s.

According to the Social Security Administration, Lisa was the number one name for newborn girls in the United States throughout most of the 1960s. Suddenly it seemed that every parent of a new baby girl was calling their sweet bundle of joy Lisa.

As the decades passed, Lisa lost favor. By 2016, Lisa had dropped to 833rd on the name popularity list; that year, only 342 newborn girls in the entire United States were named Lisa.

The New York Times Magazine even ran an article entitled "Where Have All the Lisas Gone?"

This phenomenon is not particular to Lisa.

Research in fact shows there is often a bell-shaped curve to describe the popularity of a given name, one that illustrates when names first come into favor, reach a peak of popularity, and tumble to relative obscurity.

Why is it that things—and not just names—fall in and out of style?

Feeling Exposed

During World War II, Robert Zajonc escaped from a German labor camp. Recaptured, he was sent to a prison in France, where he escaped again and joined the French Resistance.

But this is less a story of a famous escape artist than it is a narrative about one of the world's most revered social psychologists. After the war and armed with a well-deserved sense of confidence, Zajonc decided to study psychology. He ended up earning his Ph.D. at the University of Michigan, and devoted the rest of his life working to understand what drives human behavior, publishing many foundational studies on the topic.

One critical experiment Zajonc conducted was in 1968 at the University of Michigan. He recruited students and told them they would be participating in a language-learning experiment. But this was just a cover for his true intentions.

He began by showing the students fake Chinese characters that he claimed signified various adjectives. Next, he proceeded to show each character to his study subjects at various frequencies. Some characters he kept to himself, and others he showed as many as twenty-five times. Finally, Zajonc asked each volunteer to guess how positive or negative the definition of each adjective was (that is, did it represent a good trait or a bad trait) and how much they "liked" it.

Keep in mind that the Chinese characters Zajonc was showing

his study subjects had no meaning whatsoever. They were made up. But what Zajonc found would have a seismic impact on our understanding of people's tastes and preferences. He discovered there was a near-seamless linear relationship between familiarity and how positive people thought something was *and* how much they liked it. The more often someone had seen a fake Chinese character, the more they preferred it.

In other words, mere exposure to one of the Chinese characters made the respondents in the study perceive it more positively. Zajonc later called this phenomenon the *mere exposure effect*. His findings have since been well documented across a wide variety of fields, ranging from nonsense words (yes, this is the actual academic term) to art and advertising. The more familiar something is, the more we like it.

If seeing something more makes you like it more, how can we use that to create hits? I'll explore that further in the pages ahead. But first, I wanted to understand the *why* behind the mere exposure effect. Why does this vivid pattern occur? To answer this, I talked to a researcher at the University of Virginia who studied the mere exposure effect in a more serious context: racism.

The Learning Potential of Racism

Racism often seems like an unsolvable problem.

The United States fought a bloody war over slavery, and nearly a century later hundreds of thousands, if not millions, of people marched in the 1960s in protests against institutionalized racism. Yet today, racism is still part of the global dialogue. From structural racism, to implicit bias, to explicit prejudice, societies all across the globe have been unable to rid the world of racism.

What if neuroscience could, if not help reduce racism, then at least help us understand it?

Researchers Leslie Zebrowitz and Yi Zhang at Brandeis University wanted to understand whether Zajonc's mere exposure effect could be used against race-based biases. What would happen if they showed respondents the faces from other ethnicities over and over?

As part of their study, they decided to focus on the orbitofrontal cortex, which is tied to the reward system of our brains. It drives two different reflexes that help our brains assess a situation before we take action. Specifically, the orbitofrontal cortex's role is to tell us whether we're better off approaching or avoiding a person, place, or thing.

Consider first the approach reflex, which can be measured by observing activity in our brains' *medial* orbitofrontal cortex. When this area of the brain is activated, your motor system eggs you on to engage with someone or something. As Dr. Zhang put it, "In a gambling setting, if you start to win money, the medial orbitofrontal is where it activates the most because it registers positive rewards."

Next, consider the avoidance reflex, which scientists measure by observing activation of the *lateral* orbitofrontal cortex. When this region is activated, our brains tell our bodies to run away to avoid the possibility of a negative outcome. The stronger the activation, the more pronounced the feeling. Still using the gambling example, Dr. Zhang explains, "When you start to lose money, the lateral orbitofrontal is the region that activates more because that's when you feel bad about the situation."

Still, the question remains: How does the mere exposure effect work? As we are exposed to something over and over again, does our approach reflex increase or does your avoidance reflex decrease? Or as Dr. Zhang puts it, "Is it because we start to feel better about those stimuli or is it that we start to feel less bad about them?"

To find out, Dr. Zhang and her team conducted an fMRI study of 16 white men and 16 white women. An fMRI machine is different from an MRI machine, as the former lets the scientist see the changing activations in the brain by measuring blood flow. It can show where activations are happening, while a traditional MRI shows only the size of the various parts of the brain. Each participant was exposed to pictures drawn from a collection of Black faces, Korean faces, written Chinese characters, and random shapes. These pictures were shown different numbers of times to the study participants, with some pictures never shown and others shown many times.

Next, the researchers put each participant into the fMRI machine and exposed them to forty images they'd never seen before and twenty they had. The idea was to see how and where the brain would react.

What the scientists found was that for the images the participants hadn't seen before—the unfamiliar ones—the avoidance reflex in their brains was activated. Simply put, people were afraid of the unknown. More than just for faces, this same effect occurred when respondents were exposed to unfamiliar shapes and Chinese characters.

It seems that humans have evolved to fear the unknown because it signals potential harm. If an early caveman spotted an unfamiliar species of red lizard under a bush in the forest, they might have been tempted to eat it. But over the millennia, evolution has primed our brains to signal avoidance, as that same lizard could in fact be lethal. Today the sight of an unknown lizard triggers our avoidance reflex and make us want to race back to camp rather than eat the red reptile.

However, simple *familiarity* reduces this avoidance. Consider that the study subjects' avoidance reflex was significantly reduced when they were exposed to the same faces, shapes, and characters they'd seen before going into the fMRI machine. The more we're exposed to something, the less we fear it.

Dr. Zhang also observed another surprising effect. "What we found is that once our participants have been exposed to a pro-totypical Korean face, they start to show less adverse reactions to other faces in the same racial category."

Familiarity was actually able to reduce race-based biases.

So what about the approach reflex? Interestingly, with increased familiarity, it neither changed nor increased. Familiarity does not make us like things more. Rather, it makes us fear things less.

This is one reason why we typically enjoy our own home. People and objects that are familiar feel safe. We may not particularly like that old chair we inherited from our grandmother—it's not that great to sit in and it clearly needs to be reupholstered—but it gives us comfort to have it around.

Back to an earlier point, though. If it's true that familiarity breeds comfort, why did the name Lisa lose popularity over time? Why wouldn't more and more parents name their daughters Lisa, until one day we all woke up living in Lisaland?

Love Kills Slowly

Don Ed Hardy was a tattoo artist who for years was best known for the Japanese-inspired designs he inked on bodies at Tattoo City, the San Francisco studio he opened in 1977.

One day he got a call from Christian Audigier, the business-man behind the trendy Von Dutch clothing brand. Audigier had seen one of Hardy's designs and wanted to take it mainstream. He asked Hardy about signing a license to build a brand around his art.

Hardy researched Audigier and, as he later told one interviewer, "This guy is at ground zero of everything that's wrong with con-temporary civilization."

Nonetheless, the desire for greater exposure won out. "I just wanted to get paid and to be left alone." In short order Audigier got the master license of Hardy's artwork and brand.

Audigier embarked on a deliberate strategy of getting celebri-ties to wear the new Ed Hardy brand of clothing. He wanted the brand to become the epitome of Hollywood chic and be seen by all.

The particular marketing strategy led to one of the biggest fads of the decade. In 2009, it was impossible to turn on the television without seeing a celebrity wearing a T-shirt plastered with skulls and mottos like "Death Before Dishonor" and "Love Kills Slowly."

Very suddenly, Ed Hardy was a household name. That same year the Ed Hardy brand sold $700 million in clothing and acces-sories.

Familiarity had created a fortune.

The Novelty Bonus

Have you ever noticed that when the new iPhone comes out, the old one suddenly seems less attractive?

If you are more comfortable with things that are familiar, why would this be? Shouldn't everyone be carrying vintage iPhones from 2008? Or pink Motorola RAZR flip phones from 2004?

Another study conducted by Zajonc provides the answer. Za-jonc teamed up with several other researchers to investigate how his mere exposure theory works in the art world. As people see a painting multiple times, will they continue to like it more, the same way Zajonc's original respondents did when exposed to fake Chinese adjectives?

First, imagine you saw this abstract painting as you made your way through an art museum.

Now imagine you had to walk by it five more times. Do you think seeing it repeatedly would change your opinion of the work? What if you saw it ten times? Twenty-five times?

Seeking an answer to this question, the researchers showed reproductions of different paintings, like the one above, to students either zero, one, two, five, ten, or twenty-five times.

The students were asked to pay the closest possible attention to the paintings. Afterward, they had to rate each painting on a seven-point scale, from "I dislike it" to "I like it."

If you recall Zajonc's original study, you might expect that with every additional view, the preferences of study subjects would increase as they unconsciously grew to fear the painting less.

Instead, the paintings that the students had seen twenty-five times were about 15 percent *less* liked than the ones subjects were seeing for the first time. In short, the students preferred the novel paintings more than the ones that were familiar.

In this case, exposure *reduced* their liking for the paintings.

This goes against the previous Zajonc study. In this newer study, novelty was preferred to familiarity.

Why were the results different?

To understand this, one first has to delve into the role of the brain neurotransmitter dopamine. Dopamine is one of the most misunderstood and, frankly, overhyped chemicals in the brain. Avid readers of pop psychology books or any books sold in airports have undoubtedly heard mention of dopamine, as it is generally portrayed as the "pleasure neurotransmitter." Countless keynote speakers have suggested companies need to trigger dopamine in their customers' brains to drive gratification and addiction.

But this view of dopamine isn't strictly true. In contrast to what the popular media might have us believe, dopamine plays a much more nuanced role in the human brain.

To find out more, I called Emrah Düzel, a neuroscientist at the Institute of Cognitive Neuroscience at University College London, known for his study of motivation.

Düzel explained why the popular notion of dopamine makes no sense. You can prevent dopamine activity in someone's brain and they will still find pleasure in things. When researchers block the dopamine receptors of drug addicts, the addicts still consume, enjoy, and crave drugs. So what's really going on?

"Dopamine is not so much about the pleasure of consuming something, it's about the motivation to obtain something that's signaled by dopamine," Düzel explains. The actual role of dopamine in our brains, he says, is to determine when we should *approach* something to learn more about it. Düzel explained that dopamine signals to our motor system that we have to *do something*—and only then does it trigger the learning process. Dopamine, in short, is not the pleasure neurotransmitter; it is the *motivation* neurotransmitter.

Düzel wanted to study what the role of novelty was on our brain's dopamine levels. To do this he partnered with fellow British researcher Nico Bunzeck for a multistep experiment.

First, Düzel and Bunzeck showed volunteers a series of photos of people's faces. The volunteers then went inside an fMRI machine, where they were exposed to even more pictures, including images they'd seen before mixed with novel, never-before-seen images.

Bunzeck and Düzel next measured the responses in the motivation center of respondents' brains, known as the midbrain, which plays a significant role in determining dopamine levels. The more the motivation center of our brain is activated, the higher our dopamine levels and the more motivated we are to explore and learn.

What Bunzeck and Düzel found was that novelty activated the brain's motivation centers. Novelty releases dopamine and encourages us to pay attention and find out more about what's in front of us.

Why?

Imagine that you are a prehistoric cave dweller who comes across a field you've never seen before. It would benefit you from an evolutionary perspective to be motivated enough to explore this unfamiliar territory, as it could be a new source of food. Scientists call this a "novelty bonus," and it's why we pursue and enjoy novel things, whether it's a new car, phone, or food. Thus the activation is the brain's reaction to the potential rewards that may or may not exist whenever we confront novel situations and objects.

But now we're faced with an obvious contradiction: We are motivated by novelty, and also fearful of the unfamiliar. How then do we balance our interest with our apprehension? Part of the answer can be found by visiting a psychology lab in Canada. There, a team of researchers decided to see what happened when people were forced to listen to the same song over and over.

The Creative Curve

Researchers at the University of Toronto and the University of Montreal were curious to understand how the contradictory fear of the unknown and the pursuit of novelty worked in music.

Does the mere exposure effect exist when we sit down and listen to a song? Professor Glenn Schellenberg, the team's lead researcher, explained to me why, prior to the study, he thought it might. "Often you hear something, and it's only in the second or third listening where you say, 'Oh, I like that song.'"

He also wanted to figure out what role novelty and overfamiliarity play in our love of, or aversion to, a piece of music. Especially the latter. "We were interested in being able to document another phenomenon, the one that people get really sick of music after they've overheard it, you know, like, the 'Macarena' or, I guess, 'Hotline Bling.'"

Put more bluntly, why do we learn to love certain songs and get sick and tired of others?

In an attempt to answer this question, Schellenberg and his team placed 108 undergraduate students in a soundproof booth alongside a computer and a pair of headphones. The team then played the students half a dozen song clips. The team didn't just use each clip once—they played two clips thirty-two times, another two clips eight times, and the last two clips twice. Afterward, the students were asked to rate how much they liked each clip, and also weighed in on various clips they'd never heard before.

If you believe that our brains pursue novelty at all times, you would also expect that every time students heard a song, they would like it less and less. At the same time, if you believe that people fear the unknown and crave what's familiar, this means that every time students heard the song, they should have loved it more and more.

But neither happened. When listening intently to the music, the students' enjoyment of the music followed a bell-shaped curve. From the second to the eighth time they were exposed to each song, the students reported liking it *more*. From the eighth time to the thirty-second time, they liked the song *less* every time they heard it. Similar to the results of Zajonc's painting experiment, by the final time they heard a song they actually liked the song noticeably less than they did when they first heard it.

It turns out that the human pursuit of both familiarity and novelty results in a bell-shaped curve relationship between preference and familiarity. We like songs more and more with each additional exposure until they reach a peak, at which point they become overexposed. From that point on, each additional listen makes us like them less and less. I call this bell-shaped curve *the creative curve*.

The Creative Curve

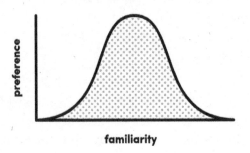

The creative curve describes a personal phenomenon, tied to one person's familiarity, so what happens when an entire population of people is exposed to a particular song, movie, or product? This is where the study of trends becomes important.

A Dose of Reality

Don Ed Hardy found out about the power of trends the hard way.

He told the *New York Post* that, at the peak of his brand's popularity, "It got surreal. I would go into a store to get a magazine and see an Ed Hardy lighter. At one point, there were seventy sublicensees."

After 2009, however, the popularity of Ed Hardy clothing plummeted. Suddenly Ed Hardy shirts were a gaudy cliché.

Don Ed Hardy believes that the reality star Jon Gosselin's obsession with wearing the brand on the show *Jon & Kate Plus 8* was the final blow. "That's what tanked it. Macy's used to have a huge window display with Ed Hardy, and it filtered down and that's why Macy's dropped the brand."

By 2016 the brand was gasping for air.

How did a brand climb as high as it did, then tumble so far down?

Google provides researchers with a tool that shows the number of people who search for a particular phrase over time. It's a good way to observe and time some of the country's, and the world's, most popular trends. What happens when we plug in the words "Ed Hardy"?

Beginning in 2005 and peaking in 2009, the brand underwent a dazzling rise. Then it all came crashing down.

Worldwide Google Searches for Ed Hardy

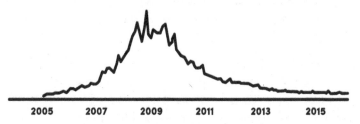

Notice anything? It's *another* bell-shaped curve. It turns out that while the creative curve maps an *individual's* preference, it also shows a *group*-level effect. As various people are exposed independently to something at different rates, overall the group at large, the masses, reflects the same behavior. For example, in clothing, fashionistas see brands earlier than mainstream people, but they also tire of them earlier. The result is that around the same time a mainstream individual is just starting to get interested in Ed Hardy, the so-called "hip" people are already tired of it.

The Ed Hardy brand, along with the name Lisa and countless other phenomena, became so popular that it reached what I call the *point of cliché*, where novelty seeking peters out at a group level, the brand in question becomes overexposed and overfamiliar, and each additional exposure reduces a group's overall interest in the product, idea, or concept.

The Creative Curve

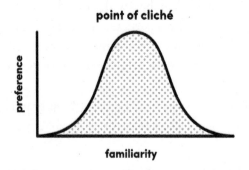

Understanding both the creative curve and the point of cliché is critical to knowing how to achieve mainstream success. You want ideas that are familiar enough to increase the chances of widespread adoption, and that at the same time create enough of a "novelty bonus" to drive interest. Think back to the "fro-yo" craze that peaked in 2011. Fro-yo was similar to ice cream, both visually and texture-wise, and therefore familiar. But it was also tart-tasting, and supposedly healthier for you than ice cream, making it novel and different. Consider, too, the popularity of the "sushi burrito" trend (enormous sushi rolls that you can eat with your hands) that appeared coast to coast. Sushi is familiar to many, and the sushi burrito was simply a novel twist on something we already recognize. This, and other ideas, are successful because they're rooted in what we already know, but intriguing enough to stimulate our brains' "approach" region.

Thanks to the widespread cultural belief in the inspiration theory of creativity, many people believe that the key to popularity is to come up with innovative, radically novel ideas. The problem is, this can result in ideas that are too far to the left of the creative curve. These ideas aren't well timed. They are *too* new, *too* different: they're not familiar *enough*. A novelist risks ending up with a book no one likes, a songwriter with a melody everyone hates, and a start-up with no users. In the best case, you're Herman Melville writing *Moby-Dick,* a work that failed to resonate with readers until decades after the author's death. In the worst case, you spend years creating something radically innovative that almost no one is interested in. A good novel needs more than novelty; it also needs familiarity.

This is true across *all* types of creativity.

André Bishop is the producing artistic director of Lincoln Center Theater, and to date the recipient of fifteen Tony Awards. *Vanity Fair* has called him the "Perfect Gentleman of New York Theater." He and I met in his office off the labyrinthine hallways concealed within the Lincoln Center complex. Bishop looks like a man who wears a suit to any and all functions. He's dapper, in the most traditional sense of the word.

He explains how timing is essential in theater. "Certain plays and musicals hit the zeitgeist at the moment." He gives an example: "I think a show like *Hamilton*, especially when it first arrived, hit the zeitgeist of what was going on, especially in New York. That simply wouldn't have happened fifteen years ago."

This doesn't mean that *Hamilton*'s success comes down only to timing. Bishop explains that a good play or musical also *must* be "written by a first-rate writer, directed by a first-rate director, beautifully cast with excellent actors, and scenery that fulfills the aim of the play."

Key to understanding commercial success, then, is understanding the nuances of the creative curve. Good execution is necessary, but it's not enough. Success requires that any creative work resonate with today's audience, otherwise you will wait for an audience that may never appear.

When Less Is More

In early 2004, a social network was launched at an Ivy League university. Created by students, it was among the first social networks to use people's real names. It spread like a contagion. Seeing the potential, the team took a leave of absence from their studies to focus full-time on the start-up.

But this isn't the story of Facebook.

It's the story of CampusNetwork, a social network launched at Columbia University mere weeks before Facebook became a phenomenon at Harvard.

CampusNetwork was cofounded by Adam Goldberg, the class president of the School of Engineering, and Wayne Ting, the class president of Columbia College. Not only was CampusNetwork launched a few weeks earlier than Facebook, it was also dramatically more advanced. The original version of Facebook was little more than a virtual directory, complete with pages devoted to basic profiles, friends, and "poking." Many of the features that would eventually make Facebook a media disruptor, such as photo sharing, the wall, and the activity feed, came much later.

CampusNetwork not only started with photo-sharing and a wall where members could comment on their friends' profiles, its activity feed made it possible for anyone to see what was happening across the entire network, just like Facebook's future News Feed feature.

After going live in the spring of 2004, Goldberg and Ting moved to Montreal to work full-time on CampusNetwork, while the Facebook team moved to Silicon Valley to do the same. In the fall, the CampusNetwork team embarked on an all-out war against Facebook, launching the site in other Ivy League schools while also making forays into Big Twelve schools, which at that point had never heard of Facebook.

Along the way, school papers picked up on and began devoting articles to the rivalry. Once CampusNetwork launched at Stanford University, *Stanford Daily* asked one student, Eva Colen, about the differences between the two. Facebook, Colen replied, was inferior: "There is no community whatsoever, it's more like a classifieds section . . . You can build relationships and express your personality on CampusNetwork, whereas [Facebook] only allows you to add friends and stalk crushes."

But for all its advanced features, CampusNetwork stalled and ultimately failed. Outside of Columbia University, Goldberg and Ting weren't able to compete seriously against Facebook anywhere. Eventually, feeling defeated, Ting returned to school in the spring of 2005, and Goldberg joined him the following semester.

Why did CampusNetwork flop? Why aren't the names of Adam Goldberg and Wayne Ting emblazoned in the public consciousness? If the site offered more advanced features from the start—ones, I might add, that later contributed to Facebook's enormous success—why did they not work for CampusNetwork?

It comes back to the creative curve.

Wayne Ting's start-up experience gave him valuable perspective on how consumers welcome—or dismiss—new ideas. Looking back, Ting now realizes that the sheer density of features contained in his app, which he assumed would leapfrog CampusNetwork over Facebook, was actually a core reason it failed.

How, though? Ting told me that at the time, people held radically different views about digital identity and privacy. In the early 2000s, we still used pseudonyms and nondescriptive usernames online. CampusNetwork asked users not only to put aside pseudonyms and use their real names, but also to share photos and updates with their network.

Says Ting, "We were asking them to make too many leaps at once."

Facebook, by contrast, added more features in a gradual way as users became more and more comfortable sharing information online. David Kirkpatrick, a technology journalist and the author of *The Facebook Effect*, remembers how barren early Facebook was. "It was essentially nothing other than a place to put a profile and to connect with other people." Ting once told a BBC interviewer, "What Facebook did that was incredibly smart was to hook them with the friending and the poking, and then they learned with their users, and added functionality slowly over time as users became more comfortable."

In essence, without necessarily being aware of what they were doing, Mark Zuckerberg and his Facebook team were following the creative curve. They were balancing the familiar with the novel. Something *too* novel risked scaring people off—whereas something too familiar wouldn't drive any interest.

In David Kirkpatrick's book *The Facebook Effect*, Zuckerberg is quoted as telling the author that "the trick isn't adding stuff, it's taking away."

CampusNetwork cofounder Adam Goldberg agreed, "Facebook trained their audience to use the site very slowly without being overwhelming."

Over the next few years, Facebook slowly rolled out more and more public social features. Occasionally there was pushback in response to a new launch, for example, when the site rolled out its News Feed. The new feature shared users' Facebook activity with their entire social network. The public nature of this caused a public relations backlash. But Facebook persisted. In fact, Facebook had a secret ingredient that helped them master the creative curve: data. As David Kirkpatrick explained to me, users may have been complaining about the News Feed, but *they were complaining about it on the News Feed*. "Time and again, they would see that usage data contradicted what users said. They might protest a new feature, but they used it."

Matt Cohler, one of Facebook's first five employees, and later a VP of product management there, explained during a lecture at

Stanford in 2008 that one of the unique things about Facebook has been that audience usage went *up* year after year. Usually, consumer start-ups shed users over time as they became less novel. But Facebook's usage metrics consistently increased, in part because Facebook pushed new features that were at the right point of the creative curve. These innovations were familiar enough to feel comfortable but at the same time novel enough to pique continued interest and encourage user engagement.

Looking back on the experience, Ting feels mixed emotions. "I think it's really hard not to look at this with some amount of regret, and maybe some amount of jealousy.... How often do you get brushed by a billion-dollar idea?" On the other hand, he and Goldberg also feel a lot of pride. Ting continued, "Even if you are just a minor bit player in the history of social networking, we played a part."

What would have happened if CampusNetwork had launched its app with fewer features? After all, it had a head start, a smart Ivy League team, and a determination to grow. It's hard to answer that question, but we do know this much: CampusNetwork didn't altogether understand what its audience wanted. It didn't grasp the creative curve.

Being able to balance familiarity and novelty isn't just useful for creating fortunes, it is essential.

Getting Fluent

The question is, how and why did users eventually come to accept Facebook's modules? Why did the exact same features that sank CampusNetwork later help turn Facebook into the juggernaut it is today?

You can break it down like this:

As we discussed, when we first come face-to-face with something novel—a book, a TV show, an app, a radically new antiperspirant—both the approach and the avoidance reflexes are activated in our brains. The unfamiliar makes us fearful—it may well harm us—but our desire to explore and learn about new things is *also* triggered at the very same time.

When most of us experience something new, for the first few encounters our avoidance reflex (*"Run away!"*) overwhelms our desire to approach (*"Check this out!"*). The result for most of us is that we back away, the goal being to protect ourselves from whatever that new thing is.

This means an idea that is *too* novel has a much harder time appealing to a broad audience. It may well appeal to fringe communities—think hipsters in Williamsburg or goths in suburban malls—but the mass population of suburban parents won't go near it.

Over time our avoidance reflex is activated less and less often as we learn that the new thing won't harm us. At this point, the novelty bonus begins to outweigh our avoidance reflex. Our fear begins to dissipate. We start wondering if this new thing, or experience, could potentially be useful or valuable.

Once this happens, we start to express liking that thing increasingly every single time we see or experience it. This upward slope is what I call the *sweet spot* of the creative curve. Ideas in this region of the curve are familiar enough to be comfortable, yet novel enough to compel our ongoing attention.

Eventually, as the novelty bonus deteriorates, we become less and less interested in what's in front of us; after all, we can no longer gain a potential big reward. As Dr. Düzel, who carried out the dopamine experiment, explained to me, "Once you learn about an environment and it becomes familiar, then the novelty bonus decays over time." Which is another way of saying that it reaches the point of cliché.

Is there life after the point of cliché? Yes, but it's the equivalent of the dark side of the moon. After reaching the point of cliché, many ideas become what I call a *follow-on failure*. If you opened a

The Creative Curve

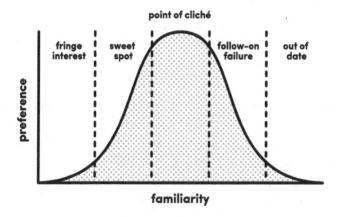

cupcake shop in 2015, soon after the cupcake craze had peaked, yes, you might have had one busy year, but very likely you will soon experience a sudden drop in popularity, if you haven't already.

Finally, once an idea is out-of-date and no longer popular, it is nonsensical to pursue it. If you opened a store devoted to disco in early 2018, you may well have attracted a tiny audience of cultural laggards, but nothing more. The individuals who ultimately become known as creative geniuses know to abandon ideas long before they ever reach this point.

Technology Adoption Cycle

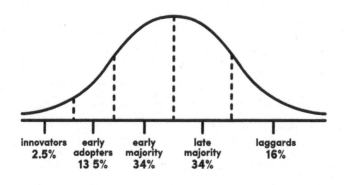

It's worth noting that the creative curve shouldn't be mistaken for another famous curve, the technology adoption cycle. (In this model, as time passes, technology goes from zero percent adoption to 100 percent.) There are two fundamental differences between the two. For one thing, the creative curve is based on exposure, rather than on time. Second, creative ideas start as unpopular, become successful, then end up unpopular again. Seldom if ever do creative ideas remain at high popularity, unlike useful technology (such as the zipper) that remains (nearly) universally adopted.

By this point you might be wondering, if the creative curve is able to explain how the tension between familiarity and novelty affects our preferences, how then are we able to account for the original Zajonc experiment I wrote about earlier with the fake Chinese adjectives, where study subjects professed to like those characters more and more with every additional exposure?

In response, researchers have two explanations. The first is that the experiment might have been lacking enough exposures to trigger the boredom effect that we see in the downward slope of the creative curve.

The second and more likely explanation is that researchers believe that *how* you and I process a concept is vital to how we learn to like—or dislike—it.

For example, in the Canadian music study mentioned earlier, it turned out that the bell curve happened only when students were asked to listen to the music *intently*. If the music was played faintly in the background, the students often kept on liking the song more and more as they heard it over and over again, with no apparent end. So why is this?

It turns out that when we consume something superficially, whether it's an advertisement, song, or work of art, our brains process it in a different way than they do when we consume something in depth, or over time. A process that neuroscientists call *perceptual fluency* takes hold. It works like this: The first time we see or experience something, our brains have to work hard to process it. However, if we've already experienced that thing, we are naturally more fluent in it, and our brains can process it more efficiently. The thing is, typically we tend to confuse this ease of processing with actual *liking*. When you think about it, it's a lot easier for us to process a song we've heard overhead in the supermarket or drugstore a hundred or so times. Along the way, we tend to mistake ease with actual enjoyment.

Advertising researcher Christie Nordhielm has studied this effect in advertising. She found that if a print ad repeatedly displayed a small or superficial feature—a background, say, or a logo—people reported liking the product in question more every time they saw it. This is why marketers deem logos and brand colors as essential to creating and maintaining consumer goodwill. The little things make it a lot easier for our brains to process the advertisements we see every day—and the ease of mental processing often gets mistaken for actually *liking* that toothpaste, aftershave, or insurance company.

In contrast, Nordhielm found that if she asked respondents to examine these same ads *carefully*, the creative curve kicked in. After viewing an advertisement ten times, the participants reported liking the underlying products less and less with each viewing.

When you process things deeply, you take time to evaluate them, and your competing emotions involving familiarity and novelty come into play. Deep processing takes place either because you are intentionally paying close attention to something, or because the object or concept is inherently complex and requires more-than-normal processing. For example, abstract art demands significant mental processing by its audience because of its multifaceted nature (there is both explicit and implicit meaning)—and is therefore subject to the creative curve.

But the creative curve isn't just an academic tool. It provides a practical framework for navigating the tension between the pursuit of both the familiar and the novel. Put simply, it is the very real foundation of mainstream success.

The question remains: How do some creative people achieve consistent success at creating ideas in the sweet spot? How are they able to come up with one idea after another that sits to the left of the point of cliché, with optimal odds of becoming a hit?

To answer this, let's go back to Paul McCartney and the Beatles.

The Math Behind the Beatles

It was 1965 and Beatlemania was in full bloom.

And while McCartney toiled to finish "Yesterday," the other Beatles were seeking ways to grow artistically while under a burdensome microscope of global fame.

George Harrison thought he had found an outlet on the set of their film *Help!*. The movie's plot pokes fun at the idea of an Eastern cult that was vaguely Indian. It was in this setting that George Harrison made a discovery that changed pop music.

In one scene, which takes place in an overdone "Indian" restaurant, a group of musicians begins serenading the diners using traditional Far Eastern instruments. At one point during production, Harrison picked up one of the prop instruments. It was a sitar, a twelve-stringed instrument that resembles the guitar.

The sitar was well known across India but completely new to Harrison. Ironically, at the same time that the Beatles were making fun of Indian culture in *Help!*, Harrison became intrigued by the mesmerizing twang and sheer foreignness of the sitar.

Seeking as ever to build his own identity within the group and continue to grow artistically, Harrison came to the conclusion that the sitar could bring about some much-needed change for himself, both musically and personally. Back in London, he bought his first-ever sitar at Indiacraft on Oxford Street.

That October, the Beatles got stuck completing a new song called "Norwegian Wood" for an album they planned on calling *Rubber Soul*. Finally, they thought to try out Harrison's new sitar. The melody clicked. Today "Norwegian Wood" is remembered as the first mainstream Western song to feature a sitar—but not the last.

As the song gained in popularity, the sitar began popping up elsewhere. In 1966, the Rolling Stones used it in their hit song "Paint It Black," solidifying the instrument's new role in rock music. By 1967, the "sitar craze" was sweeping pop music. Danelectro went so far as to release an electric version, known as the Coral electric sitar. This version of the sitar was accessible to many musicians; it was strung like a guitar but had the recognizable twang of an actual sitar. The trend kept going, and more pop musicians began incorporating the instrument, ranging from Elvis Presley to the Mamas and the Papas.

That same year, Harrison met Ravi Shankar, one of the godfathers of Indian music, and a master of the sitar, who eventually agreed to teach Harrison how to play the instrument. Shankar, on tour in 1967 during the sitar craze, told an interviewer that the sitar "is now the 'in' thing." All of which he credited to the Beatles and Harrison's abrupt obsession with a movie prop. "Many people, especially young people, have started listening to sitar since George Harrison, one of the Beatles, became my disciple."

The Beatles had lit the match, but the ensuing fire consumed musicians everywhere. As it threatened to burn higher and higher, the Beatles began cutting back on the sitar. It ended up just being one of many new sounds the band used during their more experimental years.

The sitar craze is a powerful example of the calculus behind the creative curve.

Any Beatles fan knows that there were distinct phases to their musical career. Many Beatles historians would classify them into three eras: the early years, which were dominated by a pop sound; the experimental years, when their music became more psychedelic and sonically oriented; and the later years, which represented a return to the pop basics.

Professor Tuomas Eerola at Durham University researches

empirical musicology. Put simply, he studies the quantitative characteristics of music, such as how many beats a song contains or the frequency of note repetition. In the late 1990s, he set out to understand whether the Beatles' phases were truly distinct: Did the phases in their music suddenly stop and start? Or were the shifts gradual, slowly evolving between albums?

To study this, he examined, among other things, the Beatles' use of tone repetition, descending bass lines, and exotic instruments like the sitar. He then measured the use of these features in every Beatles song ever recorded.

What he found was that the Beatles used these experimental features with an increasing, and then decreasing, frequency. When Eerola created a chart showing this change over time, you can probably guess by now what shape he saw—a bell-shaped-curve distribution.

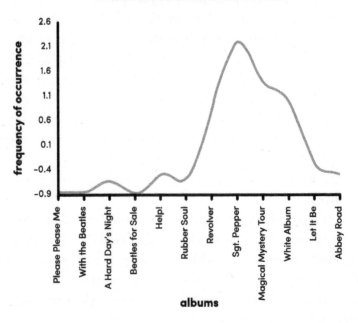

Experimental Features in Beatles Albums Over Time

The Beatles' usage of experimental song features matched the creative curve. The band slowly introduced an increasing number of experimental approaches and sounds in their music as their audience grew to like them, then stopped using them as their audience risked becoming overexposed to these sounds.

Part of the Beatles' creative genius was their ability to write songs that mirrored how their audience built new musical tastes, which follows the creative curve. The band wrote and released songs that were familiar yet just novel enough to expose their audience to new concepts that listeners would slowly learn to like. Then, once these elements reached the point of cliché, the Beatles sharply curtailed their use.

Imagine what would have happened if instead of reducing these musical features once they reached cliché, the Beatles had continued. Their fans would have begun to get bored, and might have drifted away to other bands. In the worst-case scenario, the Beatles might have become a cliché themselves.

The creative curve provides the framework to explain how the Beatles could bring new ideas to the market and find success, without carrying those ideas too far, or staying with them too long.

This has critical implications for any type of creator. For example, one way to slow down the effects of the curve is to slow down exposure. That is why many luxury brands focus on exclusivity, maximizing price to grow revenues rather than distribution. The only other way to avoid the curve is to make your product addictive (think of the staying power of coffee or certain videogames).

Yet, how did the Beatles know how much sitar to use in their music? Alternately, how did Mark Zuckerberg know which features to take away from the earliest versions of Facebook?

Here is where my interviews became critical. I sat down with dozens of successful creatives from numerous fields. My goal was to understand how they managed to generate one idea after another at the sweet spot of the creative curve. Since we all have creative potential, and extreme IQ genius is *not* a requirement for creating hits, I wanted to map out these individuals' creative process. What were *they* doing that the rest of us should consider replicating?

I asked these people questions about their childhoods, how they conceived of new ideas, how they turned those ideas into reality, and how they promoted them once they were done. I often felt like a shrink, especially since I conducted a lot of interviews on couches. People invited me into their homes, their offices, and their favorite restaurants. When we couldn't meet in person, we would chat over the phone or Skype.

In the end, it turned out that many of the stories I heard were similar. Ultimately I discovered four patterns that creators use to come up with ideas that are optimized for commercial success. These methods were also supported by a variety of sciences ranging from psychology to sociology to neuroscience. I call these the *four laws of the creative curve*. Over the next four chapters, I'll break down each one, and explain how we can apply all of them to our own work.

We'll start by discussing how to *identify* great ideas.

And, as you will soon see, it all begins with a trip to Arizona.

Part II

The Four Laws of the Creative Curve

Law I: Consumption

It was 1982, and Arizona Video Cassettes West was packed with customers. The checkout line snaked back past the Comedy section, through Horror and into International. The store was one of the first video rental stores in Arizona, but that wasn't why customers were willing to wait in line for twenty minutes or longer.

If you had asked the men and women why they were standing there, their reply would have sounded nonsensical. They were all waiting in line to talk to the clerk: Ted. More to the point, many of them had spent all that afternoon thinking about what question they would ask him.

Why?

Ted was an eighteen-year-old community college student. To earn extra money, he worked at Arizona Video Cassettes West, stocking shelves and checking out rentals.

Ted's childhood was chaotic. His parents were just teenagers when his mother had him, and before long, he had four additional siblings running around their small house in the Phoenix suburbs.

To escape the disorder at home, Ted took to visiting his

grandmother's house, where he would watch endless hours of television. Ted's grandmother loved show business, which was reflected in the piles of entertainment magazines overflowing on every surface and piece of furniture. She enchanted Ted with stories about the actors of the day, referring to them by their first names as if recalling old flames. For Ted, movies and television became the ultimate escape from his own chaotic household.

Not only was Ted's household in perpetual disarray, but so were the family's finances. His parents loved to spend money they didn't have, and any earnings his parents brought home were quickly spent on new gadgets and electronics. Though the landline would be disconnected from time to time because of unpaid bills, Ted's was one of the few families in the neighborhood to already own a VCR.

One day, when Ted was biking around town, he noticed a new shop in one of the local strip malls: a video rental store. Thanks to the VCR his parents owned, and the time he spent with his grandmother, Ted had grown up loving movies, so the new video rental store was a fantasy come true. Ted went inside and started chatting with the storeowner, Dale Mason, who was behind the counter wearing a tracksuit (this was the 1980s, after all). Ted soon learned the man's life story.

Dale had been an air traffic controller in Chicago before deciding to become an entrepreneur. He had read a magazine article that predicted that yogurt shops and video stores would be the biggest businesses of the decade. "I hate yogurt and love movies," he told Ted, and his path was set. Dale soon moved to Arizona, where he was able to afford both a house and a small retail space.

Over the next few days, Ted returned to the video store, spending hour after hour in conversation with Dale. The two of them talked about movies as Ted made his way around the store, organizing the shelves for fun. It was clear Ted felt completely at home amid hundreds of videos, and it took Dale no time at all to realize he had found a kindred spirit. He offered Ted a job as a clerk and Ted accepted, happy to be surrounded by VHS tapes.

Most video rental stores were empty during the day; customers typically rented movies after coming home from work. Rather than doing his homework during his quiet shifts, Ted made a pact with himself that he would watch every single movie in the store. He wanted to learn everything he possibly could about films, and finally he had the best possible resource—a well-stocked video store—at his disposal.

A few months later, after watching nearly every movie on the store shelves, Ted had morphed into a human recommendation engine. If you were a customer who liked Woody Allen films, Ted would suggest you try the movies of Albert Brooks, announcing that "what Woody Allen is to New York, Albert Brooks is to L.A." Like a particular action movie? Ted had three other movie suggestions that would keep your blood flowing in just the same way.

Ted, in short, had developed *cultural awareness*, a real-time consciousness of what is familiar, what is good, and what is cliché. It is this skill that allows someone to identify where exactly an idea or product falls on the creative curve.

By going on a consumption binge, Ted, at age eighteen, had become a movie expert—a film sommelier, in other words. He understood what made people tick, and customers, aware of his insight about what to watch, and wanting to benefit from his perspective, were willing to wait—and wait—to talk to him. Similar to the restaurant critic whom diners trust to point out the best new places to eat, individuals with this type of awareness are valued in society. We seek them out. We refer to them as tastemakers and influencers. We even promote them to leaders in companies and in our culture.

Cultural awareness—being able to identify where an idea falls on the creative curve—may appear to be out of most people's reach. While the food critic, the hip artist, and the successful mobile app founder all understand consumers, it's hard to imagine how the rest of us could gain that same skill.

The thing is—we can. In this chapter, we'll explore how and why *consumption* can enable you to learn this skill. And we'll learn how this can also be used to *purposefully* increase the number of "aha" moments you have.

Is It Luck?

Some entrepreneurs appear exceedingly lucky, especially the ones who create multiple successful businesses, sometimes even across multiple industries.

Entrepreneur Kevin Ryan, for one, founded nine Internet companies, including the media company Business Insider (acquired for $450 million), online fashion powerhouse Gilt (acquired for $250 million), and database technology company MongoDB (valued at over $1.5 billion). Not only that, but he was part of the early team and served as CEO of the advertising technology pioneer DoubleClick, which was eventually acquired for over $1 billion. From e-commerce to media to database technology, Kevin Ryan is a serial entrepreneur with a shockingly good hit rate.

Another successful serial entrepreneur is Martine Rothblatt. As a young lawyer, Rothblatt became fascinated with satellites, and cofounded Sirius Radio. Today, in the wake of its merger with XM radio, SiriusXM is valued at over $25 billion. Yet when her daughter was diagnosed with pulmonary hypertension, a lethal and incurable disease that affects the lungs, Rothblatt left Sirius Radio and decided to reinvent herself. After taking courses in biology, she founded United Therapeutics, a biotech start-up devoted to creating treatments for pulmonary hypertension and other, similar lung diseases. Today, United Therapeutics is a public company valued at over $5 billion.

Whereas most people would struggle to create even one great

business, Ryan and Rothblatt have created multiple runaway successes. More impressive still, they were able to switch industries along the way, while still achieving extraordinary success. Was it merely genetic luck? Or could there be something else at work?

Professor Robert Baron, who studies the intersection of entrepreneurship and psychology, wanted to understand how entrepreneurs ferret out opportunities.

The answer, he found, is pattern recognition.

One of our brain's fundamental tasks is identifying patterns. This task is critical in helping both to protect us and to discover rewarding opportunities. As we discussed, if something poses a threat to us, we want to avoid it. If something promises a potential reward, we want to explore it.

Pattern recognition relies on two mental models, both of which Professor Baron believes are used by entrepreneurs to come up with new ideas.

Coffee Shop Prototype

The first is a *prototype*—but not the kind of prototype that might immediately come up in most people's minds. In psychology, a prototype is an abstraction of any concept's fundamental properties. Think of a coffee shop. A prototype, in this case, would be a small storefront that sells coffee and muffins, has tables, and (depending on how benevolent the owners are) offers free Wi-Fi. Or, in a business context, a prototype of a tech start-up would be a young, high-growth-rate company that raises venture capital and offers, it believes, some sort of unique technology.

Early on in their careers, entrepreneurs rely heavily on prototypes to guide their decisions. They often absorb these prototypes from books and from the advice of colleagues. For example, let's say an inexperienced entrepreneur, Mike, is interviewing a job applicant, Tom. Mike would probably use a "successful employee prototype" (someone who is resourceful, curious, responsible, smart, etc.) that he has ingested from outside resources to assess who Tom is and what he could potentially bring to the company. Mike would have to think carefully about whether or not Tom matched these prototypical characteristics. It is a slow, thoughtful process for identifying the familiar.

The second mental model is the *exemplar*, which is basically a specific example of a category. Adam Sandler, for example, is an exemplar of a comedian. Mention the name "Adam Sandler," and people would categorize him instantly as a comedian. This doesn't mean he's the funniest comedian around (a touchy point in many circles), but instead that he is a specific comedian against whom you can compare others. The same goes for "Christmas movies," an exemplar of which would be *It's a Wonderful Life*.

As entrepreneurs gain experience, most start to accumulate concrete examples of a variety of concepts, and over time they rely more and more on exemplars. Using exemplars speeds up idea processing. After all, entrepreneurs don't have to slow down and recognize the individual, distinctive elements of each and every new idea that's presented to them. Most simply accept that this or that new idea matches an exemplar and is familiar. Let's go back to Tom, our aspiring employee, and imagine that he's being re-interviewed by an experienced entrepreneur, whom we'll call Sally. Sally has worked with numerous people in her career, good and bad, and these colleagues and friends have become, for her, exemplars. Sally would automatically compare Tom to the best, or most promising, employees she's worked with in the past, and upon deciding that Tom in some ways is similar to a former star colleague, she quickly offers him a job.

Exemplar Model

One critical facet of pattern recognition is that it allows entrepreneurs to develop an uncanny instinct for opportunity. Research shows that when entrepreneurs have significant prior knowledge, they no longer need to engage in slow, deliberate searches for new ideas. On the contrary, their prior experience gives them a rich library of exemplars they can access automatically. Experienced entrepreneurs recognize valuable ideas that are familiar to them based on *previous* valuable experiences.

In short, thanks to exemplars, intentional learning and experience make entrepreneurs far more likely to discover a useful new idea, as they can efficiently recognize what is familiar to the exemplar.

Earlier I mentioned serial entrepreneur Kevin Ryan, a successful participant in numerous companies across the tech industry. Kevin has learned to make use of exemplars to find new ideas. He told me how he came up with the idea for Gilt. "On Eighteenth Street in New York, I walked by two hundred women waiting in line. I asked one of them why they were all lined up like that and they told me it was all for a Marc Jacobs sample sale." Kevin was instantly reminded of an exemplar: Vente-privee, a French website that sells discount luxury goods, allowing customers to avoid traveling and waiting for sample sales. Spying the line, he realized this was potentially more than just a European phenomenon. What about the thousands of other potential customers who loved Marc Jacobs, but couldn't make it to New York City that day, or hated waiting in lines?

In short, he observed something familiar to a successful exemplar.

Another example is Jared Polis, an American politician and entrepreneur and one of the richest members of Congress. According to financial disclosures, he is worth somewhere *between* $184 million and $591 million (the U.S. government likes to keep things "broad"). Polis made his fortune as an Internet entrepreneur. While attending Princeton, he launched an Internet ISP that was later acquired for $23 million. Next, he founded Blue Mountain Greetings, which was acquired during the first Internet boom, this time for $760 million in cash and stock. He even started a flower company, ProFlowers.com, which went public and eventually sold for $430 million. As if that weren't enough, he also founded a charter school network and cofounded the high-profile start-up accelerator TechStars.

Today, though, Jared Polis is mostly known as a quirky congressman (he is a devoted turtleneck wearer and an active video gamer) who is currently running for governor of Colorado. We talked on Skype one night about how he used to discover new business ideas.

As the research we discussed has shown, the combination of experience and knowledge makes recognizing new ideas more or less "automatic." One day Jared was sending flowers to a friend, and was taken aback by the price list. *Why were flowers so expensive?* He had no experience in agriculture or in the flower business, but he also knew what a good business looked like—not this!—and knew many companies, exemplars, that had benefited from moving to a direct-to-consumer model.

He trekked around the country, studying the supply chain, "I visited growers and flower markets. I visited distributors. I talked to tons of industry players." His mission was to understand where during this whole process prices exploded.

The result was a completely new model of flower company. ProFlowers sent flowers *directly* from the grower to the customer, no middlemen or resellers needed. This enabled ProFlowers to deliver fresher flowers for lower prices, creating hundreds of millions of dollars in value—all from an idea that ostensibly appeared in a sudden flash.

Experience makes generating familiar ideas easier, but what happens if you don't have experience? Well, there is another way that entrepreneurs can develop exemplars and prototypes. Creative people can also use intentional consumption—see Ted, our video store clerk—to achieve similar results. We don't need direct experience to develop prior knowledge. It turns out *observing* something can be nearly as good as developing exemplars and prototypes.

Studies have found that successful entrepreneurs focus on ingesting third-party material that is specific to the field they work in. One study found that members of a particular entrepreneurship hall of fame were more likely to find inspiration for new business ideas from reading niche trade and industry publications, in contrast to typical entrepreneurs nationwide. Exemplars don't come from consuming just *any* information. They arise from consuming highly relevant material either within an entrepreneur's field or a field they're considering entering.

Through voracious consumption, serial entrepreneurs can develop a set of valuable exemplars—even when they switch to new or unfamiliar industries, as Kevin Ryan and Martine Rothblatt both did. These exemplars in turn allow them to identify promising new ideas.

A New Perch

Over the years, and especially today, Ted Sarandos has continued to consume an enormous amount of material, in his case roughly three to four hours of film and TV a day. But he does this from a very different perch: a corner office in Beverly Hills. Ted is now the chief content officer of Netflix, where he has overseen its transformation from a DVD rental business to an original programming business that has already won more than forty Emmys, with hit shows like *Stranger Things* and *Orange Is the New Black*.

But let's go back a few years, to when Ted dropped out of college to become the general manager of the same video store chain he was working for. This led to an executive role at a video distribution company, and in 2000 he was offered a position at Netflix leading all content acquisition. Looking back, he describes his video store clerking days as "film school and an MBA course all wrapped up in one."

Today, working for a company known for its recommendation algorithm, Sarandos jokes, "I guess I was using an algorithm years before I even knew what an algorithm was." Consumption had driven his ability to understand an audience and create content they cared about.

By taking in enormous amounts of material, Ted is today the possessor of a vast library of exemplars. This gives him the ability to process new pitches and ideas efficiently, and recognize immediately whether they're original, borrowed, different *enough*, *too* different, or somewhere in between. Because of this, Ted and his team have the ability to identify content that hits the ideal spot on the creative curve. It's content that has, as Ted describes it, "one foot in familiarity and one foot in something really fresh, unknown, and novel."

A Surprising Principle

Finding ideas that are familiar to an audience is one of the underpinnings of commercial creativity.

From my interviews with today's successful creative artists, I found a surprising pattern. Ted Sarandos's mass consumption of movies, and the focused, industry-specific consumption of other leading entrepreneurs, weren't flukes at all. No matter whether I was interviewing a painter, a chef, or a songwriter, I'd eventually hear some variation of the same story. Painters show up at numerous art exhibits. Chefs eat at cutting-edge restaurants, visit farms, and travel to food shows. Songwriters are constantly listening to music, new and old.

Although these creative artists are typically wildly busy, they consistently spend three to four hours a day—that is to say, roughly 20 percent of their waking hours—on this type of consumption. This kind of experience allows them to develop the exemplars necessary to know where an idea falls on the creative curve, as if by gut feel.

I call this the *20 percent principle*: by spending 20 percent of your waking hours consuming material in your creative field, you can develop an intuitive, expert-level understanding of the level of familiarity of an idea—where it lies on the creative curve—even without real-world experience.

As I explained earlier, studies show us that to master a craft we need to invest in countless hours of purposeful practice. The

20 percent principle is different from that: it won't enable anyone to create the perfect omelet, play the violin, or shoot a basketball. The 20 percent principle isn't about the physical act, or about muscle memory. Rather it enables us to identify the *ideas* that are appropriately familiar. We still need to call on the skills to *execute* those ideas (or hire the right people who can), but the 20 percent principle provides the initial electricity for our light-bulb moments.

In short, the 20 percent principle allows you to access the creative curve. In order to create content that is familiar, creative people typically call on an extensive base of knowledge. If you're a writer, it's critical to know what books in your category the audience has read and liked. If you paint for a living, you need to understand whether your latest piece lands on the correct point of the creative curve, or whether it risks coming off as trite, passé, or, alternatively, hopelessly avant-garde.

Consumption provides the fuel. But how do you turn that fuel into conscious ideas?

Digital Mogul

Connor Franta looks like most hip L.A. twentysomethings: tight pants, a designer-y T-shirt, and an omnipresent iPhone.

A native of Minnesota, he is someone most people wouldn't look at twice if they passed him on the street. But if he walks by a group of teenage girls, you will hear shrieks, and you might even see one or two faint.

Franta is a YouTube celebrity who started posting videos in 2010, when he was only seventeen years old. Today he has more than five million subscribers on his page, with each video typically receiving over 500,000 views.

He has also written two *New York Times* bestselling memoirs, and launched a clothing line, a coffee brand, and a record label with a Sony distribution deal that specializes in pairing emerging musicians with powerful social media influencers.

Franta has become a new type of digital mogul, something he credits to his ability to understand his audience: "I know what I like and I've found, through the years with YouTube, that people like what I like."

How did a teenager from Minnesota gain this ability?

Again, it started with consumption.

"Before I even made YouTube videos, I was a viewer," Franta explains, "I watched tons of YouTubers, and in a way, studied them and just understood YouTube before I got into it myself."

Like Ted Sarandos's, Franta's consumption helped him develop a sense of what is familiar to his audience. "Videos that always gained traction for me were anything I could find that was a relatable topic to anybody, or especially to the majority of my audience. I found that people always wanted me to talk about relationships or anything that was relatable to a teen."

The other thing Franta realized was the huge role that novelty played in his success. It wasn't enough to merely understand his audience and what broad types of videos they would relate to. No, he had to offer a novel twist.

On his side was timing. Many of the simple, relatable video ideas he came up with were inherently innovative. Back then, YouTube was a new frontier, Franta explained. "There were no rules. I had to set the standard." By consuming lots of videos, he knew what his audience had seen, and not seen, which cleared the way for him to create original, but recognizable, content. Without knowing it, Franta was making use of the creative curve.

Among other things, Franta created a series of video lists, for example, "10 Things to Say to a Boy You Like." These videos hit the target for his tween and teenage audience, and proceeded to rack up millions of views. Since then, Franta's videos have been copied by thousands of other YouTubers.

So how deliberate—and conscious—is the process of coming up with ideas?

The creative people I talked to, like Connor, were often aware of the mechanics that it took to develop and sharpen their consumer instincts. Nonetheless, they still talked about the resulting aha moments as if they were magical.

Like Paul McCartney, Connor Franta describes his creative process in terms of sudden inspiration. "Honestly, any idea I get, it just happens. For a YouTube video, if I go to a coffee shop after this, I'll probably get an idea there because I'll see something happening, or maybe I'll get a clothing design idea because I'll see some pattern in the sky, and I'll literally jot it down. It just happens."

His is a consistent experience across multiple fields. One day last year I traveled to suburban Maryland to meet with José Andrés, the celebrity chef who, along with his business partner Rob Wilder, owns over twenty high-end restaurants around the world. In addition, they own a fast-casual chain, Beefsteak, and a Spanish packaged goods line, and have earned two Michelin stars for their food-laboratory-restaurant hybrid named minibar.

I pulled up in front of an ultramodern house at 9:00 a.m. sharp and was greeted by Andrés's assistant. As I heard the floorboards creak upstairs, I realized I was now guilty of waking up a celebrity chef. Before long, Andrés, who has a thick Spanish accent mixed with the fast-talking locution of a kid on a playground, was ushering me into his kitchen.

We sat down at his counter and dove right into the topic of creativity. "The beginning of creativity is like the Big Bang. Why did it happen? We still don't know."

He looked up, "Anybody want coffee?"

He proceeded to take out a food scale to carefully measure out the perfect amount of espresso.

As we got back on task, Andrés explained how, like other creators, he absorbs information about his field. He likes to attend chef conferences where he can observe the latest techniques and learn everything he can about new ingredients.

To hear him tell it, the inspiration for his recipes also comes in sudden flashes.

Says Andrés, "I have never liked the salt rim on a margarita, it's usually too much." One day he had an idea. He and his wife were on vacation, lying on a beach. "As we were watching the waves crash into the shore, I thought about how light and salty those waves taste on your lips. And it hit me!" A longtime user of Sucro, a powdered emulsifier that creates interesting foams for his dishes, he thought suddenly, what if he emulsified salt? "No more salt on the rim!" Andres went on. "Just the salty sea foam, floating on top of your margarita."

In that moment, the now popular salt air margarita was born.

Andrés, like the other creative people I interviewed, experienced true moments of what felt like mystical flashes of inspiration. But if the creative curve offers a defined blueprint for consumer taste, why do these aha moments occur? Why isn't creativity more of a conscious process? And, more important, can we all learn to create aha moments in our own lives?

Being Subtle

Imagine you are in a large room. Objects are strewn about here and there, among them a chair and a table, on which there sits a pole with a hook on one end, a wrench, and an extension cord.

On one side of the room a long cord hangs from the ceiling to the floor. Another cord of the same length is hanging by the opposite wall.

No, this isn't a scene from a horror movie. It's the setting of a classic psychology study.

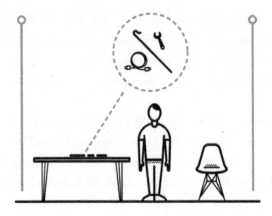

The question researchers asked participants was simple, at least on the surface: "Can you tie the two cords together?" The question is challenging, largely because of where the two cords are placed. For example, if a participant grabs one cord and walks it as far as he can in the direction of the other cord, he just can't reach that far.

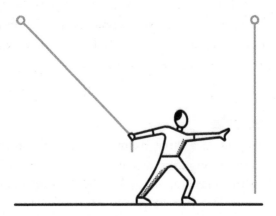

The participants were told they could use any item in the room that would help them, and also any technique that came to mind. Can you figure out a solution? (The truth is, there's more than one.)

If you came up with one or more answers, congratulations. Most people struggle. Now before patting yourself on the back, I have to break some news: there are *four* solutions in all. As a participant came up with one solution, one of the researchers would step forward and tell them, "Now do it a different way," until they uncovered all four.

Here's the first: you tie one cord to a heavy object, maybe the chair, and bring it between the two cords. Now fetch the other cord, and bring it over.

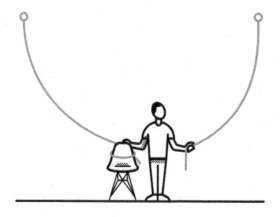

Here's the second: you can use the extension cord to lengthen one cord, before walking it over to the other cord.

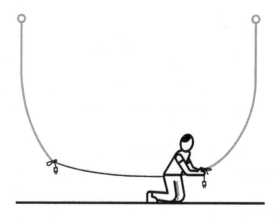

Third, you could use the pole to pull over one of the cords while gripping the other.

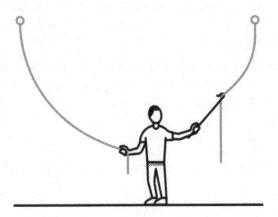

Fourth, you could tie the heavy wrench to one of the cords and turn it into a pendulum by swinging it. Then, as that chord swings back and forth, you could, again, walk the other cord over.

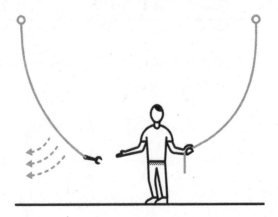

This last solution is the one that intrigued the researchers the most, as it involved a kind of transformation: you had to turn the cord into a new object, a pendulum. Of the four solutions, this one was the least intuitive.

Only 40 percent of the study's participants were able to figure out all four solutions without any assistance.

If ten minutes went by and the subjects hadn't yet figured out the fourth solution, the researchers began dropping hints. The first hint was subtle: a researcher would enter the room as if he was simply crossing it and subtly brush the cord so that it started swinging.

This hint prompted many of the participants to come up with the last solution. On average, it took them less than a minute after the subtle hint was given for them to come up with the answer.

The strange part is that only one student *consciously* made note of this subtle hint. Even when told later about what the researcher had done, the other students claimed that the brushed rope and the subtle swinging had no effect on their discovery! No, most claimed that the solution involving the wrench merely dawned on them in a moment of, well, you might call it *inspiration*.

Even though the participants weren't aware of it, the subtle hint resulted in an aha moment.

The two-cords experiment shows us two things. First, solutions often show up very suddenly in the guise of aha moments. The second and more important point is that even when these sorts of solutions "feel" like a sudden flash of genius, there is often a reason why we come up with them. They might not have been aware of it, but those students were unconsciously swayed by the subtle swinging of the cord.

This has big significance in our exploration of creativity. If scientists can prompt an aha moment in a study subject, is there a way that we can create them in ourselves?

The Science of Aha Moments

I want you to take a moment to study these three words:

Can you think of a single word that could be put next to all three and still make sense?

The answer is "ice" (ice cream, ice skate, ice water).

If you came up with the solution, how'd you do it? Did it pop into your head instantly, or did you pore through various possible solutions? If you didn't get it at all, what was your approach as you tried to figure it out?

These kinds of word puzzles tend to fascinate scientists because, depending on the person's experiences, they can be solved either through *logical analysis* or via *aha moments*.

Logical analysis is straightforward: You ponder whether a word "works" and think through the puzzle logically, step by step.

Aha moments are the flashes of genius we've talked about throughout the book. With these solutions, the answer to the puzzle would come immediately upon seeing it or after a delay, but without conscious thought.

Since these kinds of puzzles can be solved using either approach, they give researchers insights into the science of aha moments.

Edward Bowden is a researcher at the University of Wisconsin–Parkside. Bowden, along with a team from Northwestern University's Creative Brain Lab and Drexel University, sought to understand the neuroscience behind aha moments. Were they truly a magical experience, or was there perhaps a biological explanation for them?

As part of their study, they tasked subjects to solve various of these word puzzles while connected to an EEG (electroencephalography) monitor, which can quickly detect the moments when electrical activity takes place in the brain, or an fMRI machine, which as a reminder, is the machine that can pinpoint *where* brain activity is taking place by measuring blood flow in the brain.

Bowden and his team hoped that by using these two machines they could see both *when* and *where* the brain was activated during aha moments.

When connected to the EEG machine, the participants wore goggles that revealed one of the word puzzles, and were given thirty seconds to solve it. Once they came up with an answer, they were then asked whether or not the solution came as an aha moment or as the result of logical analysis.

Fifty-six percent of the answers were attributed to an aha moment, 42 percent to logical analysis, while the remaining 2 percent checked neither box. On the surface at least, there seemed to be a minimal difference between these two methods; regardless of which one was experienced, the solutions showed up roughly ten seconds later.

But the EEG readings told a very different story.

Electrical brain waves in the gamma band are thought to be activated when our brains engage in perception and language. It's one of the brain waves the scientists were most interested in studying.

When participants solved problems via flashes of genius, there was a burst of gamma band activity 0.3 seconds *before* they came up with an answer. The researchers believe that this burst in electrical activity signals when the solution enters a person's consciousness. It represents the "aha!"

This means aha moments exhibit their own unique brain wave pattern. Have you ever looked at a crossword puzzle question and were unable to come up with a solution? Then, very suddenly, the answer hits you? Well, this feeling of being struck with a sudden solution is reflected by the activity in the gamma bands.

So *where* exactly *did* the solution come from?

To find out, Bowden and the team of researchers repeated the experiment while monitoring the subjects using an fMRI machine.

What they found was that when participants reported aha moments, activity showed up in the right hemisphere of their brains. Not only do flashes of genius have a unique electrical pattern in the brain, they also have their own discrete location.

It may be a cliché to talk about the "left brain" and the "right brain," but at the same time, it's critical to our understanding of where creative ideas originate.

Generally speaking, the left hemisphere of our brains is where we process the dominant meanings of things. This is where we retrieve straightforward or contextually relevant definitions of words or concepts. When someone asks us what color the sky is, the left hemisphere of our brains shouts out, "Blue!"

The left hemisphere is also where logical analysis processing occurs. For example, our left hemisphere is activated when we're asked to solve complex math problems. Why? Because solving for x asks that we bring specific relevant concepts to the forefront of our consciousness before we work through a step-by-step solution. This often feels like a slower process, as we consciously have to work at something.

The right hemisphere of our brains is where we store more metaphorical associations. Studies show that our right hemisphere is activated when we hear jokes that, say, rely on puns, or when we try to make sense of metaphors. The right hemisphere processes problems by searching for associations between seemingly different concepts with underlying commonalities. This process is subconscious, meaning we're not aware when our right hemisphere is at work, searching for connections. Sometimes it moves quickly, for example, when we hear a standup comedian's routine and automatically know why it's funny (or not funny). Other times, our right hemisphere keeps working through a problem subconsciously, discovering a solution only much later. Since the right hemisphere operates below our general level of awareness, when it does come up with an answer, we're seldom aware of the effort it took, which is why we often experience this processing as more automated.

As Bowden explains, "The right hemisphere is processing language all the time just like the left is, but what we're saying is that the structure of the two hemispheres is slightly different and that connections in the left hemisphere are shorter, stronger, and to more direct associations while the connections in the right hemisphere are longer, weaker, and to more distant associations. If I say 'worm,' you might consciously think 'fishing' and 'earthworm'—a left-hemisphere activation. But in the right hemisphere, when I say worm, you might think fishing and earthworms, but also 'bookworm' and 'gummy worm,' and even 'earworm' [a song that gets stuck in your head and repeats endlessly]."

We don't consciously switch between processing in our right and left hemispheres, either. Instead, our brains process problems in *both* hemispheres at the same time, the difference being that, as I mentioned, the processing of our right hemisphere generally operates beneath our level of conscious awareness. We don't even realize our brains are doing what they're doing—which is why all this unseen work ultimately leads to what we think of as aha moments.

Researchers believe there are three origins of such aha moments.

The first are what I call *shower moments*. In this scenario, you might already have a solution to something in your brain's right hemisphere, but the activity in the left hemisphere is crowding it out. Once the left hemisphere's logical processing fails to deliver an answer, its activity tends to fade. Once the left hemisphere's activity falls below that of the right hemisphere, the answer from the right hemisphere pops up as if by magic. Aha!

This is why when we wake up, go out for a run, or take a shower, we often experience what feel to us like "flashes of genius." Generally these are occasions when our brains aren't overwhelmed with thoughts, the result being that we experience what seems like sudden inspiration. But if you want to know the truth, it's really just the result of our brains being empty of the crowded chaos of our left brain thinking, which in turn allows long-percolating right brain ideas to make their appearance.

The second origin of aha moments is through *combination*. Here, your brain's right hemisphere, knowing that one single concept is unable to give a satisfactory answer, is subconsciously working to connect multiple concepts. If your right hemisphere is able to braid together what feels like a workable solution, it becomes activated. It's this sudden burst of brain activity that creates that flash-of-genius feeling.

As we learned from the two-cords experiment, the third origin of aha moments involves a *trigger*. In this case, an environmental factor subconsciously ignites an association with something already stored in your brain's right hemisphere. For example, if we get stuck working on a crossword puzzle and an hour later walk past the word we were seeking on a billboard, we may well experience a flash of genius without even being aware we saw the missing word.

All three of these methods happen below the average human being's conscious level of awareness. Is it any surprise, then, that these solutions often feel mystical and sent from above by some benevolent deity? In reality, it's not magic, it's biology. Bowden explained that aha moments are simply "a normal cognitive process but they have a surprising result."

Latte Art and Brain Processing

Now I want you to imagine that you are sitting in a crowded coffee shop with a friend.

You're drinking an exquisitely crafted cappuccino—somehow the barista sketched a heart into the foam—and catching up on life.

At the table next to yours, a couple is having an intimate conversation. Even though their table is only a few feet away, you don't really hear what they're saying. Your focus, after all, is on your friend and your cappuccino.

All of a sudden you hear a person at the adjoining table utter your first name.

Just as suddenly, you can't help but listen in on their conversation for a few seconds. When you quickly realize that they're talking not about you but about someone else, you refocus on your friend and your foam heart, and the conversation taking place at the table next to yours fades into the background.

One of your brain's core competencies is its ability to filter the world around us for things that are *important*. Things that *matter*. In neuroscience, *important* is defined as something that's either potentially harmful or potentially helpful. Your brain is constantly scanning the world around you for this kind of information. When it decides that someone or something will neither harm nor help you, it quickly ignores the stimulus in question.

How does our brain do this? Well, it uses both your memories and mental models in a constant assessment of whether someone or something is a potential source of danger or reward. As I wrote earlier, it accomplishes this by gauging how familiar or novel something is.

For example, let's go back to that coffee shop. Chances are when you walked in, you didn't consciously notice the chairs. They're just chairs, after all! But what if they were exact replicas of the ones you have in your kitchen? I can almost guarantee that your attention would have been drawn to those chairs.

So how does this process of recognition work?

Bowden explains that the sight of a recognizable chair "automatically activates an existing memory instead of you having to go through and think, 'Oh, what kind of chair is that?'" The strength of this activation typically causes it to pop into your consciousness. On the other hand, if you see a chair that deviates from your image of how a chair should look, that is, the prototype, you would notice it as well, because your brain would be working hard to decide what in the world you're looking at, and whether or not it's safe.

Objects that are similar to an exemplar and objects that vary from our stored prototypes cause substantial activity in your brain.

This concept of awareness is important because it helps explain why people think that flashes of insight are magical. Since we are not aware of the work that goes into them, they feel like they take no effort.

Another reason they seem supernatural is that people report that many of their *greatest* ideas originate from, well, aha moments. When discussing their creative processes, they describe how their *best* ideas come to them seemingly out of nowhere, in places like the aforementioned shower. One survey (by a shower company, of course) found that 72 percent of consumers reported solving problems in the shower! They didn't remember the truly rotten ideas that also accompany their morning shower that their brains subconsciously discarded. All this is to say that most of us tend to correlate aha moments with valuable ideas.

I found that many of the creative people I interviewed similarly revered their own aha moments.

One evening last year, I traveled to a Greek restaurant in sleepy Malibu to have dinner with Mike Einziger. He's the cosongwriter and guitarist for the band Incubus, one of today's bestselling alternative rock bands, with over twenty-three million albums sold. Mike also writes for orchestras, serves as a producer for other musicians, and collaborates with electronic artists. For example, he cowrote the electronic hit "Wake Me Up" with Avicii, which sold eleven million copies.

That said, in person Einziger could easily be mistaken for a graduate student. With long shaggy hair, he wouldn't look entirely out of place strolling along a campus quad or studying in the stacks of the campus library. For many years, in fact, he did just that. Taking a hiatus from his life as a rock star, he attended Harvard, where he studied physics.

Einziger gave me the example of the song "Drive," Incubus's biggest hit. He had experienced a rush of inspiration where the music came to him. He then took it to his co-songwriter and lead singer, Brandon Boyd. The lyrics quickly flowed from there. "I remember sitting in my car and Brandon just sang what he sang over the top of it, and that ended up being the song," he said. The process consisted of multiple flashes of genius, giving it an almost magical quality. The two songwriters didn't argue or fight; rather this huge hit simply "clicked."

Why, though? If aha moments can be traced back to a simple biological experience, why do the ideas they generate often *feel* better than ideas that we work out via logical analysis? When I asked Bowden this question, it turned out that he and his fellow researchers at the Creative Brain Lab were eager to find answers to this same question.

Working alongside a team of Italian researchers, they employed a variety of puzzles that could be solved either by logical analysis or via a flash of sudden inspiration. They then measured the accuracy of both sets of answers.

It turns out that the reason people believe their aha moments are special is that, in fact, *they are!* The research team found that solutions generated by a seeming flash of genius were more likely to be correct than answers worked out through logical analysis.

The reason is simple (and not mystical).

Using a logical analysis approach, your brain exposes you to fragments and partial answers as it toils consciously through the problem in question. As this is happening, you are usually aware of the wrongness of your ideas, but when you're not sure of something, you may take a risk and guess. As a result, your answers aren't always correct.

By contrast, aha moments typically take place only once a complete and accurate answer is found by your brain's right hemisphere. Since we're not aware of how hard our right hemisphere is working to find answers, or of the bad ideas it subconsciously discarded, it *feels* as though aha-moment-type processing is always correct. This is why these moments are often experienced as "flashes of *genius.*"

Whether we're discussing Connor Franta suddenly getting the

idea for a clothing design when looking at the sky or Paul Mc-Cartney waking up one morning with the chords for "Yesterday," flashes of genius are far from a mystical experience. Rather, they are an ordinary process that your brain subconsciously uses to address and solve problems, and connect seemingly distinct but associated concepts. Considering that they are more likely to be correct than a solution realized through logical analysis, our culture has created a mythology around these "flashes of genius." The thing is, they're just a normal, if spectacular, function of our brains. And the best news is that they can be enhanced.

Building a Foundation

The reason the 20 percent principle is consistent among the creative artists I interviewed is that it provides the building blocks that are necessary for aha moments to flourish. This accumulation of prior knowledge fills up the brain with examples and concepts that artists then use to uncover non-obvious insights.

Bowden explained the importance of establishing prior knowledge. "I think one of the problems people have with the idea of insight is if they think it's a magical process, they think that they shouldn't have to work hard to have an insight; but what you need to do is you have to establish a certain level of knowledge. You can't have insights about things you don't know anything about."

That line is worth repeating: **"You can't have insights about things you don't know anything about."**

Aha moments tend to drive a lot of the mythology that's been constructed around creativity. At the same time, there is some truth to both their power and their hype since, as we've seen, aha moments are generally more accurate than, and superior to, normal step-by-step logical processes.

But, as a normal cognitive function, they are also something we can enhance and practice.

Want to become a great writer? Start consuming all the books you can get your hands on. Need to write better dialogue in your scripts? Start listening to people talking at coffee shops (but don't be creepy about it). Want to become a great television executive? Watch TV day and night. The 20 percent principle gives us the raw ingredients our brains need to generate aha moments. We need to have the memories and mental models for our right hemisphere to work with. Without these ingredients, we are shutting down our own potential.

This element of bulk consumption is widespread across all creative industries. Connor Franta spent years watching countless YouTube videos. Great entrepreneurs consume trade and industry material en route to identifying their next lucrative business. José Andrés visits food and restaurant conventions to observe and absorb new techniques and get introduced to the latest ingredients.

The 20 percent principle not only makes flashes of genius possible, by providing lots of exemplars, it also allows for creative people to gain insight into what will be familiar—through cultural awareness. Ted Sarandos's experience working in a video store made it possible for him to understand what kinds of stories, formats, and structures his audience would perceive as similar to other movies they loved. By understanding where an idea would fall on the creative curve then and today, he was able to lead Netflix to incredible heights in original programming.

If your goal is to achieve mainstream success, your first step should be to immerse yourself in the field you're interested in, exposing yourself to and consuming as much as possible. This will allow you to identify ideas that are familiar to previous successes.

But wait one second. Before you start consuming books, CDs, movies, or television shows, I need to point out one possible conundrum.

The fact is, many of us are already consuming massive amounts of material. According to the U.S. Department of Labor, the average American watches three hours of television every day, which comes to roughly 20 percent of their waking hours.

On the surface, aren't most American already following the 20 percent principle when it comes to gaining experience about what works and doesn't work on TV?

If we're all consuming huge amounts of television, why aren't more of us creating hit shows?

Consumption's primary role is to help you identify something's level of familiarity. But the creative curve also demands that you *create* the right amount of novelty. It's not enough to simply identify novelty; you have to add *just* the right amount. To do this, creatives consistently engage in something that may seem surprising: imitation.

8

Law II: Imitation

Beverly Jenkins was nine years old when she started walking the fifteen blocks to the Mark Twain Library at the corner of Gratiot Avenue and Burns Street on the east side of Detroit.

Growing up poor and the oldest of seven children, early on she discovered that books were a great means of escape. "Books could take you all over the world," she told me. "They could show you other people. They could show you other places. We were poor economically, but not in love, or spirit, or support, or any of that, and the books were free."

For the next seven years, she went to the library every Saturday to get new titles. When she stopped going, it wasn't because she'd lost her love for reading; rather, she had managed to read *every* book in the library.

At first, I thought when she told me she read every book in the library, she was using hyperbole to make her point. No, she was serious: "Science fiction, *Martian Chronicles*, *Dune*, nonfiction, Westerns, Zane Grey . . . I read everything in the library. Doesn't matter what it was."

Jenkins had gone through an intense period of reading that left her with an unquenchable love for both books and libraries. After graduating college, she got a job at the reference desk for a drug company, but still continued to read voraciously, especially the emerging category of romance novels that began appearing on bookstore shelves in the 1970s.

Many of the most popular romance novels belonged to the "historical romance" genre. Readers devoured stories of queens, princesses, and forbidden Victorian love. It didn't take Jenkins long to see a problem: Almost all the characters in these books were white. There were no well-known African-American historical romances. In response, she made a decision: She would create the book that *she* wanted to read. The book as she conceived it would tell the story of an African-American soldier in the all-Black 10th Cavalry during the Civil War who was in love with a rural schoolteacher.

Jenkins finished the book, but was resigned to the fact that mainstream publishers weren't exactly open to acquiring African-American-centered fiction, not then at least. One of her coworkers was also a big fan of romance fiction, and had been writing her own romance novels. When she managed to sell her book to a publisher, Jenkins, impressed, told her colleague about her own book.

The colleague insisted on reading it and a few days later told Jenkins that she needed to find a publisher *now*.

Jenkins was skeptical, but found a literary agent who began submitting the manuscript around town. After enough rejections to paper her entire home, one day the phone rang. It was an editor at Avon Books. Recalls Jenkins, "The rest, as they say, is history."

When her debut novel, *Night Song*, was published, it leapt off the bookstore shelves and into the mainstream press. *People* magazine published a five-page spread on Jenkins, and the reviews were glowing. Jenkins, it seems, was at the vanguard of an entirely new genre of books: historical Black romance.

Jenkins had produced something familiar (a historical romance novel) but different (one that included Black characters). She wrote it in an era when publishers were finally starting to bring more African-American voices into publishing. Without knowing it, Jenkins hit the sweet spot of the creative curve. Since then she has gone on to write numerous novels that have collectively sold over 1.5 million copies.

Romance novels make up over one-third of the U.S. fiction market, ringing up sales of more than $1 billion annually, making the romance genre a significant profit center for any major publisher. There are historical romances, paranormal romances, erotic romances, and many other variations, as well. Eighty-four percent of romance readers are women, and most of them are middle-aged.

That said, romance novels are often criticized as formulaic.

Sarah MacLean is a *New York Times* bestselling romance novelist who writes a monthly column on romance novels for *The Washington Post*. She is an expert in the history of the genre. She and I discussed the core elements of a successful romance novel.

First, readers expect the book or series to conclude with a happily-ever-after (or at least happily-for-the-time-being) moment. For MacLean, this makes romances more enjoyable: "The covenant that a romance writer has with their readers is that there will always be a happily-ever-after. This allows readers to lean into fear and risk while knowing that there is a safe landing at the end." The constraint gives both the reader and the writer comfort by establishing a by-now familiar baseline.

Another typical characteristic of the genre is a so-called "black moment"; there are no racial connotations, rather, this is a series of scenes or encounters where all hope is lost. The central romantic relationship of the story falls apart. Says MacLean, "Neither the reader, nor the characters, nor sometimes the writer, can see how it will all work out, and how these two will ever get together again." This often happens near the end of the book, and the rest of the story focuses on getting the characters back to where they were before. This "black moment" adds drama and suspense despite readers knowing that the characters will eventually escape their predicament. Guessing how the characters will resolve their crisis not only grabs readers' attention, it adds to a book's suspense.

Finally—and not entirely surprisingly—romance novels usually depict sex. As MacLean puts it, "Romance writers use sex on the page the same way thriller writers use murder. It drives the plot." It's difficult, she says, to write a love story without sex: "When you're in a relationship and sex happens, it's a complicated experience that changes the way a love story is told and changes the story's arc."

When readers buy a romance novel, they expect a familiar structure that incorporates the three characteristics I've just described. These recurrent features lead to the charge that romance novels are unoriginal. Beverly Jenkins disagrees. "I don't think it's any different from any other fiction," she says. "Can't have Westerns without a bad guy and a sheriff. Or a bunch of horses. Can't have mystery without a dead body and somebody trying to figure out who done it."

So, does all art rely on some type of formula?

The Cinderella Formula

Kurt Vonnegut wrote fourteen novels, including *Slaughterhouse-Five*, which immortalized him in the annals of American fiction. Yet for all his literary achievements, the work that he considered his "greatest contribution" wasn't a published book or even a short story. It was his rejected master's thesis from college.

Vonnegut was a graduate student in anthropology at the University of Chicago. Unfortunately, he hated anthropology. ("It was a big mistake for me to take a degree in anthropology anyway, because I can't stand primitive people—they're so stupid," Vonnegut once said.) But for all his animosity toward his major, Vonnegut thought highly of his thesis. At college, he had become fascinated by the emotional arc of stories. In his thesis, Vonnegut proposed that every story could be mapped out on a graph, where the vertical axis showed positive and negative emotion, while the horizontal axis signified time.

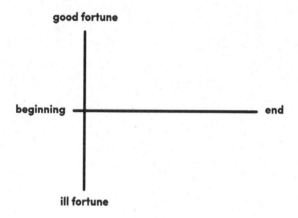

Using this chart, he began mapping out the emotional arcs of famous works. Along the way he uncovered four recurrent story types.

The first was "Man in Hole."

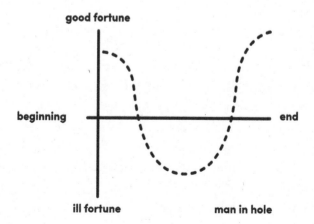

Vonnegut believed that "Man in Hole" was the most popular type of story. As he said in a lecture, "Now let me give you a marketing tip. The people who can afford to buy books and magazines and go to the movies don't like to hear about people who are poor or sick, so start your story up here [points at top of the good fortune–ill fortune axis]. You will see this story over and over again. People love it and it is not copyrighted." But the "Man in Hole" story isn't as obvious as the name might suggest. Notes Vonnegut, "The story is 'Man in Hole,' but the story needn't be about a man or a hole. It's: Somebody gets into trouble, gets out of it again [dotted line]. It is not accidental that the line ends up higher than where it began. This is encouraging to readers."

The second type of story Vonnegut found is "Boy Meets Girl."

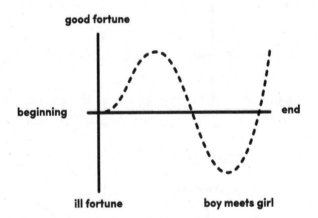

This may sound like a purely romantic story, but Vonnegut meant something broader: "This needn't be about a boy meeting a girl [begins drawing line]. It's: Somebody, an ordinary person, on a day like any other day, comes across something perfectly wonderful: 'Oh boy, this is my lucky day!' . . . [drawing the line downward]. 'Shit!' . . . [drawing the line back up again] And gets back up again."

He found two other story arcs.

A "Cinderella Story" is one where there is a rise, fall, and rise to the point of supreme happiness. More than just straightforward romances, classics including *Jane Eyre*, *Great Expectations*, and, of course, *Cinderella* all share this arc—an uplifting story that culminates with the protagonist achieving their wildest dream.

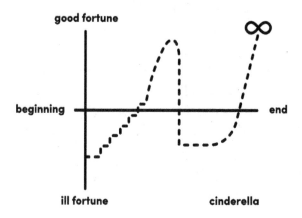

Lastly, Vonnegut identified a "Franz Kafka Story." This one is perhaps the saddest.

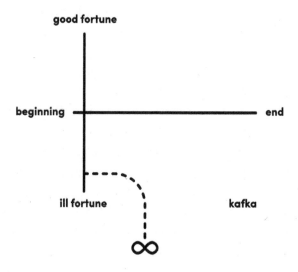

In this last category, says Vonnegut, "A young man is rather unattractive and not very personable. He has disagreeable relatives and has had a lot of jobs with no chance of promotion. He doesn't get paid enough to take his girl dancing or to go to the beer hall with a friend. One morning he wakes up, it's time to go to work again, and he has turned into a cockroach [draws line downward and then infinity symbol]. It's a pessimistic story."

Not very motivating.

These ideas reappeared in a lecture that Vonnegut gave in 1985 that later went viral on YouTube. Years later, a researcher stumbled across the video, and found that one of Vonnegut's lines was germane to the research he was pursuing. Here is what Vonnegut said: *There is no reason why the simple shapes of stories can't be fed into computers, they are beautiful shapes.*

Well, *could* the shapes of stories be fed into computers? Was there any way of proving that these stories possessed recurring patterns?

The researcher soon brought together a team of academic superheroes, experts in sentiment analysis, statistics, and computer science. Based at the University of Vermont, they decided to use some of the latest data analysis tools to see if they could uncover patterns in the emotional arcs of stories, just as Vonnegut had suggested.

To this end, the researchers downloaded novels from an online database, which also featured public statistics showing how many copies had been downloaded, which allowed the researchers to understand which books were the most popular. The team then ran the full text of these books through a series of analytical processes with geeky names ("matrix decomposition by singular value decomposition," "supervised learning by agglomerative," and "unsupervised learning by a self-organizing map"). These processes and methods enabled the scientists to create story arcs similar to the ones Vonnegut had drawn. What's more, their studies were able to detect whether a particular section of a book had a positive or negative emotional sentiment. When tracked over the length of a book, this data allowed them to map the "shape of stories"—just as Vonnegut had predicted.

Not only did the research team find the same consistent story types that Vonnegut uncovered (the difference being that the team ultimately identified six), but it soon became clear that some story types were more popular than others. The data showed, in fact, that among the types with the most online popularity was none other than "Man in Hole."

Science had proved what Vonnegut had conjectured: There *are* consistent story types that authors use in their craft. But do most writers fall into these patterns subconsciously, or are they following patterns deliberately?

To find out, we will make a detour into the world of television.

The Origin of Constraints

You may think that breakout success comes from breaking the pattern. In reality, it is only by *following* a pattern that you tap into the right level of novelty.

Black-ish is a hit ABC sitcom. To date it has run for four seasons, has an upcoming spinoff, *Grown-ish*, and has been nominated for both an Emmy and a Golden Globe as best comedy. It is the story of Dre, a father who grew up poor but is today an advertising executive. He and his wife, Rainbow, who is biracial, are raising four children. *Black-ish* explores Dre's conflicts around wanting his kids to retain their identities and heritage at the same time as they focus on assimilating with their mostly white friends. In one episode, for example, Dre's twelve-year-old son decides he wants a bar mitzvah for his upcoming birthday because he is envious of his Jewish friends.

For a work of fiction, *Black-ish* is more autobiographical than most TV shows. Kenya Barris, who created it, is the showrunner (a Hollywood term for the CEO of the show). Like the character Dre, he is married to a biracial doctor (also named Rainbow), grew up poor, works in a creative field, and has struggled to pass on his identity to his suburban children.

Black-ish is a fictionalized version of Barris's life.

I was curious to find out whether television shows had a structure or pattern similar to the story arcs found in books. Barris could help me answer this question.

People in L.A. are forever stuck in traffic and are, I find, very willing to talk on the phone about their creative process so long as neither of you minds an occasional car horn. As Barris and I spoke during his commute to work, he explained that a network sitcom episode has a traditional three-act structure, echoing the classic structure introduced by Aristotle in his *Poetics* in 335 BC.

"The first act is going to be the introduction or thesis statement of what the particular topic or thing is," Barris said. In the episode where Dre's son wants to have a bar mitzvah, the topic on the table is one of cultural identity.

Barris went on: "The second act is going to be the body, or where you deal, where you unravel, where you get into the gooeyness and funniness of what this particular issue is, and how it relates to our family and how it has an unspooling within our particular characters' lives." In that episode, the second act has Dre calling a family meeting about his son's identity crisis, and deciding that his son will instead go through a traditional African rite-of-passage ceremony.

"The third act would be the resolution, where you come to a place of what this information or what this topic or whatever the problem we put around this topic, how it's dealt with and how it lands you in a satiating place for storytelling purposes." In this episode, the resolution comes when Dre allows his son to have a hip-hop-themed bar mitzvah. He realizes that his children will have a different childhood from his, and that this evolution is simply part of life.

Why does Barris rely on this three-act structure?

Barris explains that between each of these acts is an "act break," television lingo for those "dun-dun-dun" moments you find in every show. After each and every act break, the TV show cuts to a commercial.

It turns out that television networks' advertising requirements set the structure of a sitcom. "You have to give the network three commercial breaks, plus a tag," Barris explained. (A "tag" is the short additional content at the end of most shows, after the final commercial break, which compels the audience to watch the last commercial.) "So, you have to give them four commercial breaks."

In a nutshell, Barris and his writers have an externally forced *constraint*. Their show and other shows need to fit a certain structure by mandate. This has been true since the days of soap company–sponsored television shows (hence *soap* operas). You might expect creatives to hate these structures, and see them as arbitrary rules forced on them by the establishment. Surprisingly, Barris finds that these constraints are critical to the success of any TV show. "We've been selling soap for so long that it's become part of our sort of pathos in terms of how we intake this creative process. Without the act breaks, the stories don't feel like they're being told quite the same. I think that they actually do work. They help to organize our thoughts."

These sorts of structures and patterns abound across all creative fields. When cooking, chefs have ratios. Sprinkle in too much salt and the pasta is ruined, add too much baking soda and your pastry will turn into a skyscraper. Songwriters need to make their songs a specific length for the sake of radio play. Depending on the category, writers have certain limits for how many words their books can have (trust me, this is good for readers). And, of course, on Twitter, tweets must fit within character constraints.

As I went around interviewing creators, I found that the vast majority of them enjoyed these constraints. Chefs enjoy the science behind recipes. Musicians relish the challenge of writing a song no longer than three minutes. Structures, formulas, patterns, recipes, norms, and so forth aren't a burden at all; in fact, they're widely considered tools of the craft. Later I'll explore in more detail *why* creators enjoy them, but first, let me raise a more fundamental question.

Even if creators seemingly appreciate these patterns, do their audiences?

The Science of Pop Music

Researcher Gregory Berns is a neuroscientist who found a research idea in a surprising place: *American Idol*.

Berns was watching the show with his daughter one night when he heard the contestant Kris Allen sing a cover of "Apologize" by the band One Republic.

The song sounded awfully familiar, but he couldn't figure out why.

Then it came together. Three years earlier, when he was conducting a study on musical taste, Berns put several teenage participants into an fMRI machine and made them listen to songs he had found online.

One of them was the then relatively unknown song "Apologize," by One Republic.

Berns couldn't help but speculate: Would the fMRI data he'd gathered three years earlier have predicted the mainstream success of "Apologize"?

He dusted off his old dataset. At the time, he'd tasked the teenagers to listen to 120 song clips across a wide variety of genres. Since the database he used had public data on the number of song plays, Berns could confidently ensure that the songs were reasonably unknown. After putting the students through the fMRI machine, he asked them which songs they liked the most. Berns wanted to see if there was any relationship between what songs someone *said* they enjoyed versus how their brain *reacted*.

The study yielded some interesting results. Now, though, Berns wanted to go back and see if there was any relationship between the brain reactions of his fMRI respondents and a song's future sales. Basically, could our brain predict hits?

One of the first things he did was to check Nielsen's SoundScan system, an online database of song sales, against his own dataset. He studied the three-year sales data for each of the 120 songs he tested.

As he analyzed the data, there it was! A correlation! It turned out that the brains of his subjects had a particular response to those songs that later became hits. Or in the language of neuroscience, Berns uncovered a correlation between the nucleus accumbens, a part of our brain's reward system that regulates the release of dopamine, and future song sales.

Even more surprising, the students' subjective ratings of each song were *not* correlated to future song sales, not at the time, at least. The songs that Berns's study subjects said that they liked were *not* the songs that later became hits. The students weren't able to *consciously* predict future hits. Based solely on their verbal responses, you could safely say that they hadn't the slightest idea what makes a hit song. But *unconsciously*—on a reptilian level—their brains were able to detect songs that would become future hits.

What exactly might the students' brains have been picking up on? Says Berns, "My hunch is that it's signaling something a little bit unusual, something intriguing, so maybe it's hitting the sweet spot between what you're used to, but not the same old thing."

Put slightly differently, he's talking about the creative curve.

The students were reacting to things that were familiar but with just the right degree of novelty. Earlier in this book, I explained how mass consumption gives us the tools to know what is *familiar*, but I also pointed out that familiarity alone isn't enough. In this chapter, I want to focus on providing the tools necessary to create the *novel*.

Remix Culture

As a third-year student at the University of Virginia, Alexis Ohanian had one goal: to avoid getting a "real job." He and his roommate, Steve Huffman, spent hours trying to brainstorm Internet start-ups they could create as a ticket out of the "real job" rut.

The result—eventually—was Reddit.

If you've never gone onto Reddit, you are missing out on an eclectic collection of news, adorable animals, controversial discussions, and celebrities challenging the Reddit community to "ask me anything" (AMA in Reddit-speak). Reddit, with its cute alien logo, bills itself as the "front page of the internet"—and its stats back up that claim. Reddit has over 300 million monthly active users, and according to Alexa, the website research service, it is the world's seventh-most-visited website (Amazon being the tenth). As Ohanian explained, "When it comes to the English-speaking world, Reddit is the global water cooler. It's the zeitgeist. The discussions that start there often spill over to the rest of the Internet, hours or even days later."

Among the many things Reddit is known for is the spread of memes. Memes are silly images that typically include humorous text. Many originate when someone posts a quirky image to Reddit, and the user community begins adding text to it.

Like "Grumpy Cat."

One day Bryan Bundesen was playing with his sister Tabatha's new kitten when he realized that the cat (named Tardar Sauce by Tabatha's ten-year-old daughter) had what looked like a frown on its face. He posted an image of the kitten to Reddit, where over-night the site's users made it go viral. Soon people were adding their own content to the photo of Grumpy Cat.

Grumpy Cat memes have a straightforward structure. On the top line, there is a seemingly positive or neutral statement like "A little bird told me it was your birthday." On the bottom line, there is a line of, well, what I would call, for lack of a better word, *grumpi-ness*. People across the Internet create their own variations of this template and share them with friends or on websites like Reddit and Imgur.

But the business of memes is more than just fleeting jokes.

I talked to Ben Lashes, who has a particularly millennial job: He is a meme manager. He helps develop the careers of people (and animals) who, in the ever-churning blender that is the Inter-net, go viral. He also happens to manage the three most famous cat memes: Keyboard Cat (a cat who seemingly plays a piano key-board), Nyan Cat (an animated cat whose body is a Pop-Tart), and, of course, Grumpy Cat (who, as you know, has a bad attitude). Lashes works to make sure that the creators of memes protect and monetize their brands. What endorsement deals might add to the brand value? Which ones would ruin the fun?

Lashes tells me that "Grumpy Cat is a Cinderella story for cats, because she was born in a town outside of Phoenix, in the middle of the desert, where no more than two hundred and fifty people live. She went from obscurity to people all over the world discussing her face, in detail." Grumpy Cat's Internet fame has translated into real-world fame and riches. In 2013, Friskies, the pet food company, signed Grumpy Cat to be its official "Spokescat."

I, of course, ask him the question that must be asked.

Is Grumpy Cat actually grumpy in real life?

Lashes laughs. "She is a very, very sweet cat. She's very affectionate, but it'll ruin her reputation if anyone finds out."

Over Skype, Ohanian explains that memes like Grumpy Cat not only allow any Reddit member to create potentially shareable content, but also that "memes lower the barrier to content creation. They establish certain guidelines that everyone can understand, which reduces the mental tax." With a meme, you already know 90 percent of the joke. In this case, you know that Grumpy Cat is grumpy. Ohanian told me, "What makes it funny is the ten percent twist or what the caption is. That allows many more people to be content creators who otherwise may not have been because it's a lot easier to remix an existing meme than it is to create a new one." Memes, in fact, make it easy to create content in the sweet spot of the creative curve by prescribing a familiar structure.

As we saw with Kristen Ashley and the changing gatekeepers in the romance novel category, the Internet has been instrumental in transforming the power structures of creativity. Ohanian thinks of this as the difference between top-down culture and bottom-up culture. "Top-down culture is historically what we would associate with *culture*. Historically you needed to have the means of distribution to create this kind of top-down culture. That is everything from a record company saying, 'Yeah, you know what, your music is good. We're going to get you on every radio station in America.' But top-down gatekeepers would always be surfacing culture that was being created by individuals. Some kid rapping in the Bronx was creating culture, but it wasn't until one of the institutions blessed it and basically pointed at it and said, 'Okay, we're now distributing this,' that it became 'culture.'"

For Ohanian, the success of nontraditional culture, including memes and self-published authors, is a result of audiences being able to discover these creations online. "The reality is, culture was always being created by individuals from the bottom-up but it was very narrowly filtered for the chance of distribution. The Internet democratizes that access to a certain extent. As long as you have access, as long as you have the means to use it, you now have a platform. What we're seeing on the Internet is real-time culture creation."

Whether it's top-down or bottom-up, Ohanian believes, as others before him have, that all culture is made up of "remixes." For Ohanian, creation mostly has to do with the adaptation of something familiar. "There aren't many truly original ideas. Originality and creativity are really just about clever remixes." Memes are remixes of funny images. Major movies are, too. *Star Wars* is a remix of a Western: Good guys and bad guys chasing each other, except this time they're in space! A lot of pop music, such as Paul McCartney's "Yesterday," is a remix of preexisting chord progressions, or an actual remix of a preexisting song. Chefs are often "remixing" traditional family recipes to make them appeal to a new audience.

Constraints, in fact, enable a "remix culture." They give creators the framework that ensures familiarity, while allowing them to create the 10, 20, or 30 percent that is novel or different. They allow creators to systematize the creative curve in a consistent manner, and not just as one-hit wonders.

Such formulas aren't merely a tool of convenience for creators; they are in fact the results of physiology. As I explained earlier, our brains react to specific patterns. Instead of having to guess how to tap into those biological desires, creative formulas provide shortcuts. They are reflections of countless generations of creative people working through, absorbing, and replicating the patterns of success. Ironically, constraints free up creators to *focus* on the novelty portion of the creative curve.

But simply knowing that constraints *exist* doesn't help anybody. You need to be able to learn these formulas employed by the masters. Where do you even start?

The Franklin Method

Benjamin Franklin, a future American founding father, was once a young Massachusetts resident who was ashamed of himself.

He had been writing back and forth with a friend, debating whether or not women should be educated, and his father happened to find the letters. His father wasn't upset about the topic of the debate—Ben was all for women's education, that wasn't the issue. Rather, his father was upset by the poor quality of Ben's writing. Couldn't Ben express himself more articulately?

Like a lot of us, Ben Franklin didn't want to let his father down. He made a commitment to himself to become a great writer.

To start on this path, he began reading *The Spectator*, a publication popular in coffee shops in the 1700s across England and America. *The Spectator* was known for its high-quality writing and for its pointed, well-sculpted opinion pieces on global affairs. To Franklin, it was the perfect writing model to emulate.

Then Ben had an idea: He would create an outline of an article he admired. What were the main points of each section? Once the outline was completed, he would rewrite the article using this same outline, and work to craft the right sentences. When he was done, he would compare it to the original to see how well he'd performed.

After spending some time structuring individual sentences, Franklin made his task even more complicated. He began shuffling his outline. Not only did he have to lay out each sentence, he now also had to figure out the best, most persuasive way to organize the article.

The good news? The process worked. As Franklin went through this exercise in imitation, he found his own writing getting better and better. In some respects, his own work was better than the original. Later he wrote, "I sometimes had the pleasure of fancying that, in certain particulars of small import, I had been lucky enough to improve the method of the language, and this encouraged me to think I might possibly in time come to be a tolerable English writer, of which I was extremely ambitious."

This type of imitation is something I heard about again and again from the creative people I interviewed on behalf of this book. What I call the *Franklin method* involves the careful observation and re-creation of the structures underlying successful creative work. Creators use the Franklin method to understand the formulas or patterns that have proven to be historically successful. Along the way they're exposed to a baseline of familiarity that their audience would know. Then, on top of that structure, they can add novelty while maintaining the necessary familiarity. The Franklin method isn't just a historic occurrence, or artifact. It's still a critical part of understanding and mastering the creative process in a digital world.

A Modern Application

Andrew Ross Sorkin is a media renaissance man. He created the uber-popular DealBook blog for *The New York Times*, is an anchor on CNBC's *Squawk Box*, wrote the bestselling book *Too Big to Fail*, and cocreated the Showtime hit drama *Billions*.

As with Benjamin Franklin, for Sorkin it all started with imitation.

Sorkin and I connected over Skype. He was in his Manhattan apartment, barricaded in his bedroom while his children sporadically knocked at the door. Over the occasional shouts of his kids, he told me how he built a modern media brand.

Sorkin was an eighteen-year-old college intern when he began working for *The New York Times*. He was well liked by the staff and would do almost anything to endear himself to the newspaper's reporters. When he graduated, he got a job that would be the envy of any journalism major: He was hired as a business reporter for the *Times'* London bureau. He left for England to launch his career.

There was one problem: He was still only twenty-two, with no real experience as a journalist. "I was so scared," Sorkin recalls. How do you craft stories, or even one story, worthy of the world's greatest newspaper?

Without even realizing it, Sorkin began following the Franklin method. He sought out similar *Times* stories from previous years and studied their formats. Did a story kick off with a quote? When did the writer summarize the key points? "I'd almost try to turn my own article into Mad Libs," Sorkin recalls. He began building outlines of an ideal format based on what worked, then fit his own story into that container. "I hate to say it," Sorkin says today, "but I was always trying to find the formula." The Franklin method quickly taught him the basics of great business writing, and helped skyrocket his career.

When Sorkin began writing *Too Big to Fail*, he once again followed a variation of the Franklin method. "I went to the bookstore and bought five or ten of my favorite business narratives and studied what they were doing, how did they do it, what was it that I liked about it, and what didn't I like about it." He soon discovered that his favorite books had a lot of breaks, hopping between scenes, and creating a breathless narrative. Sorkin emulated this in his own book, making it accessible and brisk. He didn't stop there. For example, he loved how the book *Conspiracy of Fools* opened with a driving scene, and how it gave the book propulsion and movement. Learning of a moment that took place in a car as he was reporting on *Too Big to Fail*, Sorkin decided to open his book with it.

For Sorkin and most other creators, standing on the shoulders of others, and seeing and mastering the patterns laid down by those creative ancestors, allows them to create exceptional work that brings together the familiar with the right twists of novelty. Imitation, in fact, helped Sorkin became familiar with creative constraints, thereby allowing him to communicate his most persuasive new ideas within a time-tested framework.

As Sorkin and Franklin discovered, these patterns are often best learned via imitation. If we imitate the people we admire, and reconstruct their past successes, we are that much closer to absorbing the patterns we need to create content at the right point of the creative curve.

Between consumption (of both knowledge and experience) and constraints, we now have a much stronger arsenal for enhancing our own creative output. These two tools can help you create ideas that are the right blend of familiar and novel, and thus in the sweet spot of the creative curve. But this only gives the *potential* for making a hit. To take an idea with *potential* and make it go mainstream takes two more elements.

As Sorkin and I were nearing the end of our video call, he made an essential point: "I was also the beneficiary of knowing a lot of those authors I looked up to or knowing people who knew them. I called them up, and I would try to almost interview them myself, and try to understand what were the great lessons and mistakes they made so that hopefully I would not do the same."

In other words, Sorkin pieced together a community of people he could learn from. As he put it, "In just about every endeavor I'm involved in there is either a partner or some person that I talk to." Whether it was his cocreators for the TV show *Billions* or his book editor, Sorkin made a habit of surrounding himself with other creative people. The public may view creators as solo geniuses, but as I spent more time with real-life creators, I found this couldn't be further from the truth.

In fact, building the right type of community might be the *most* crucial part of the creative process.

Law III: Creative Communi-ties

The popular image of the creative genius is that of a brilliant neurotic who accomplishes superhuman feats of creativity on their own. Alone. In a metaphorical cabin somewhere.

This image has filtered up from decades if not centuries of popular culture. In the *Iron Man* cartoon, and the subsequent movie empire, Tony Stark is a singular genius. He runs a massive corporate empire and builds his own robotic Iron Man suits. But this idea exists beyond fiction; Tesla and SpaceX's Elon Musk is routinely compared to Stark.

That said, it's pretty clear that the mythology around the self-reliant genius makes little sense. Elon Musk employs thousands of people who enable him to create futuristic technology. Hundreds of years ago, Mozart spent countless hours learning from his teachers, and also sought out numerous collaborators.

Even though over the course of writing this book I found that creativity is very much a team sport, our cultural mythology, at least in the United States, remains extremely focused on the individual. I plead guilty myself: Most of the stories I am telling you are about individual people, and not about the groups surrounding them.

But ignoring the social aspect of creativity has dire consequences.

Studies show that building a *community* of people around us is essential to achieving world-class success. One study from the University of California analyzed the social networks of more than two thousand scientists and inventors. The research demonstrated that an innovator's network could predict prominence, productivity, and even the length of their career.

Another study found that a wide range of world-class performers (ranging from artists to athletes), had *all* studied at one time under a relentless and experienced teacher.

Yet another study of successful artists found that the strength of an artist's reputation was correlated to the number of relationships they had with other successful artists, both within and beyond their own generations.

This is not as simple as saying you need collaborators. I found that creatives had *four* different types of people in their networks: a *master teacher*, a *conflicting collaborator*, a *modern muse*, and a *prominent promoter*. Each one of these roles is filled either by an individual or by a group of people. No role is more essential than another: with only one of these roles absent, a person's creative success becomes less likely. Together, these form what I call a *creative community*—a community of people who directly and indirectly affect a person's creative process.

These creative communities are one of the most important and yet least studied aspects of creativity.

In my interviews, I found that not only are these four roles essential, but I learned how creatives found (or attracted) these vital people.

Over the next few pages, we'll answer two critical questions: Why are these people so important and, more to the point, how can we find them?

Let's start by turning on the radio.

A Master Teacher

Taylor Swift's album 1989 has sold over 10.1 million copies to date. It has had three number-one singles and is considered one of the most successful records of the past decade.

When you think of Taylor Swift, her Coca-Cola ad might come to mind: Taylor is backstage writing her hit song "22," strumming guitar chords and scratching out the lyrics in her diary. She exhibits an organic, sweat-free creativity.

But when you scan the liner notes (or nowadays the Internet), you'll find a different story. Almost all of Swift's songs have cowriters. Her trio of number-one singles from the album? All three were cowritten by Max Martin and Shellback.

Who is Max Martin and who is Shellback (and does he really have no last name)?

You could call Martin a "hit doctor," but that would be a vast understatement of both his success and his talents. NPR once dubbed him "The Scandinavian Secret Behind All Your Favorite Songs." Martin is in fact the king of modern pop, ranking third for the most number-one singles ever, after John Lennon and Paul McCartney. These include Katy Perry's "I Kissed a Girl," Pink's "So What," Maroon 5's "One More Night," and nineteen others (though by the time this book is published, the number will have risen).

Shellback works for Martin and is one of the dozens of songwriters who either work for Martin or were trained by him in his method. For example, Martin taught Dr. Luke, who has written hits for Taio Cruz and Kelly Clarkson. He also taught Savan Kotecha, who's responsible for numerous chart-toppers for the boyband darlings One Direction. Other Martin protégés are Benny Blanco, who was mentored by Dr. Luke and is thus an intellectual grandson of Martin. Blanco went on to write number-one singles for Justin Bieber and Maroon 5.

The scale of Martin's influence is evident when you look at the Billboard number-one singles from 2014 to 2016. Over the course of those three years, there were twenty-nine number-one singles in all. Of those, 21 percent were either written or cowritten by Max Martin, and another 7 percent were composed by a Martin protégé. That means that nearly one in every three chart-topping Billboard singles was composed by a small group of friends and colleagues. Those are just the *number-one* singles. That doesn't include all the other high-performing songs Martin and company wrote that "merely" cracked the Top 10 or Top 100.

How is one small group of songwriters able to dominate a creative field?

Max Martin's talent resides not just in his great ears, but in the fact that he taught others his songwriting methods. Asked at a conference what makes a great pop song, Arnthor Birgisson, a songwriter who has written hits for Santana, Celine Dion, and Janet Jackson, and was mentored by Martin, explained that the older Swede taught him a formula. Among its elements? "Never use more than three melodic parts in a song. . . . Three parts and recycle parts of the verse or part of the song in the chorus so when the chorus comes you already heard the chorus but it's the beginning of the verse."

Max not only teaches his protégés the constraints and formulas that come together to create a familiar pop song, he also helps them perfect their craft. As I wrote earlier in my section on deliberate practice, learning from an experienced teacher and getting feedback from them is an essential step in developing and honing a creative skill.

Bonnie McKee is a lyricist who worked with Martin and many of the people in his group. She's cowritten the words to songs including "Dynamite" by Taio Cruz, "California Gurls" by Katy Perry, and countless others. Interviewed by *The New Yorker*, she said of writing lyrics for Max Martin, "It's very mathematical. A line has to have a certain number of syllables, and the next line has to be its mirror image."

Mathematics, it turns out, is a core element of writing a great pop song. Martin, in fact, has referred to his creative process as "melodic math." His reasoning is straightforward. As McKee said, "People like hearing songs that sound like something they've heard before, that's reminiscent of their childhood, and of what their parents listened to."

Or, as we would say it, they like to hear things that are familiar.

Martin also provided McKee with the feedback she needed to improve her skill. "I can write something I think is so clever," she said, "but if it doesn't hit the ear right then Max doesn't like it." Master teachers like Max Martin are essential to the creative process. What makes people like Martin "masters" is that they've achieved a level of success beyond the typical experienced practitioner. Jonathan Hardesty, the painter, found a master teacher at the atelier he attended in South Dakota. Andrew Ross Sorkin became friends with older, wiser authors.

Master teachers serve two essential roles: They teach constraints, and they assist with deliberate practice through feedback. Absorbing these constraints in turn allows students to make progress more rapidly, as they refine their own skills.

Back in the early 1980s, a researcher studied the lives of 120 high achievers, ranging from mathematicians to sculptors to athletes. The goal of the study was to trace the lives of high achievers back through their earliest years in order to uncover what common elements, if any, led to their ultimate success. The researcher's findings were published in a book, *Developing Talent in Young People*. One key finding: Across all fields, *every* individual in his study had at one time been taught by a master teacher.

So how do you attract a master teacher? Do you just snap your fingers? In search of an answer, I went to L.A. to visit a rock star turned investor who is friends with everyone from billionaire grocery store magnates to the hip-hop superstars that dominate today's charts.

Learning Patterns for Young Guns and Billionaires

D. A. Wallach is a thirty-three-year-old redhead whose mentors include everyone from Pharrell Williams and P. Diddy (whom Wallach calls Puff Daddy) to Weezer's Rivers Cuomo.

Wallach and I are sitting on the patio outside his halfway-renovated home on a foggy morning in the Hollywood Hills. I am characteristically chipper. Wallach pulled into his driveway only minutes before, and is even more cheerful than I am, laughing at all my jokes (which are not funny). Wallach is a hybrid artist-musician-investor. Before turning his talents to companies, Wallach was the lead singer of the one-time indie darling Chester French, a band formed while he was still an undergraduate at Harvard. Around the time he graduated, the band was the target of a bidding war between Kanye West and Pharrell, both gunning to sign them to their record labels.

Ultimately Wallach and his band signed with Pharrell's label, where they released the album *Love the Future*. The band eventually fizzled out, yet Wallach still remains a part of the music world. He was Spotify's artist-in-residence for a while, helping the start-up build better relationships with musicians. He also played a minor role as a singer in 2017's hit movie *La La Land*.

Alongside his musical and artistic career, Wallach has also invested in companies ranging from Spotify to SpaceX. Despite not being your stereotypical blue-dress-shirt finance type of guy, today he is a partner at Inevitable Ventures, a fund he cofounded with billionaire grocery store mogul Ron Burkle, which invests in high-growth tech companies.

How did this young former band member get connected to rap icons, billionaires, and tech unicorns?

Wallach credits a large part of his success to the people he's learned from: "It's always been me feeling someone has all the answers and then kind of latching onto them and hoping that they'll teach me." At Harvard, for example, he found out that Weezer's lead singer, Rivers Cuomo, was on break from touring and going to Harvard as a student. Wallach dug up Cuomo's e-mail in the student directory, and reached out cold to see if the two of them could meet. Soon, they were grabbing dinner at the dining hall and Wallach was learning about the music industry from one of modern rock's most famous talents.

Wallach has continued to seek out teachers, adding, "I've had a series of people I also *forced* to be my mentors." The key, he says, is learning to be curious. "Ninety percent of my day is just asking questions."

The point is, don't wait for someone to take you under their wing; initiate the process yourself. If you meet someone who is successful in a field you want to learn about, approach them. Be curious. Be relentless! As Wallach and others found out, most people are happy and willing to share their experience and knowledge. All you have to do is ask them.

Nor do you have to be young and green to need a master teacher or mentor. In fact, many of the most established people I interviewed have what are known as *reverse*-mentors.

David Rubenstein, the cofounder and co-CEO of Carlyle Group, one of the largest private-equity firms in the world, with $158 billion under management, has a reported net worth of $2.5 billion. In addition, Rubenstein sits on over thirty nonprofit boards, of which he chairs seven, including the Kennedy Center, the Smithsonian Institution, and the Council on Foreign Relations. He also hosts *The David Rubenstein Show* on Bloomberg TV, where he interviews people ranging from Oprah to Bill Gates.

We are sitting together on an outdoor patio in Aspen, Colorado, during the annual Aspen Ideas Festival, one of those big ideas conferences that lures everyone from renowned ballet dancers to financial titans. Rubenstein orders mint tea, and we discuss how he goes about learning new things. What I'm struck most by is that for a man in his sixties who has amassed billions, Rubenstein sounds remarkably similar to D. A. Wallach. "I like to meet people who are very smart, who know something about areas I don't know," says Rubenstein, adding, "I spend a lot of time asking them questions." Like Wallach, Rubenstein has a question-based conversation style; he's always pushing for more information. "It's easy for me to ask people questions, and I like to find people who can tell me something I don't know."

Soon his laser-like approach turns on me. "Do you know something I should know? You're the expert on big data."

This pattern kept reappearing in my interviews.

Kevin Ryan, the serial Internet entrepreneur we met in an earlier chapter, told me that he, too, focuses on learning from people with niche knowledge. "A successful meeting for me is when I'm speaking thirty percent of the time—because I don't learn anything if I'm speaking all the time." Ryan may have started multiple nine- and ten-figure valuation companies, but he's still primarily interested in learning from others. "I had a great conversation yesterday with the friend of my daughter who's sixteen and has a whole bunch of theories on education and different education systems," Ryan told me, adding, "You can learn from anyone."

As I continued interviewing people, I found that many of the *most* successful people I spoke to were also the most open and the most willing to create moments of learning and vulnerability.

How do you create these moments?

The best method, I found out, is to bring novel people into your orbit. Ryan, for one, accomplishes this through food. "One of the ways I do this is through dinner parties. We'll try to have someone in politics, someone from an Internet company, and some random people." If you dislike entertaining, another idea is to invite a coworker out for coffee, or simply say yes the next time some precocious college student asks to "pick your brain."

Now, if you're successful already, it can be far easier to bring people into your network. But what if you're just starting out? We can't all get into Harvard and rub shoulders with rock stars in philosophy class.*

Clustered

A young woman was sweeping the lobby of the Park Hotel in the SoMa section of San Francisco, the neighborhood south of Market Street. The lobby had muted green walls with benches that looked ripped out of a diner. It wasn't truly a hotel, rather it was affordable housing with shared bathrooms. As she continued sweeping, she noticed a photographer snapping a picture. Over thirty-five years later, the resulting photo appeared as part of a photo series on the gentrification of SoMa. Since that time, San Francisco, and SoMa in particular, has gone from impoverished to unaffordable.

Office space in the formerly rundown SoMa neighborhood now rents for an average of $72.50 per square foot (matching pricey Manhattan), and studio apartments sell for an average of over $1,200 per square foot, which means that a small 450-square-foot studio costs more than $540,000, which is enough to buy a Mc-Mansion in many suburbs. As for the Park Hotel, it has turned into a techie commune where aspiring entrepreneurs and software engineers can rent minuscule rooms for $1,000 per month.

So why are people moving there in droves?

Somewhere along the way, SoMa turned into one of the epicenters of the start-up industry. In its immediate vicinity, you'll find the headquarters of Twitter, Salesforce, Pinterest, and Zynga, as well as offices for major companies including Google, Yelp, and

---

* If you are interested in finding ways to connect with potential mentors, I put together a digital guide with a more detailed how-to. You can find it on TheCreativeCurve.com/Resources.

Adobe. As more and more tech companies migrate to the neighborhood, more people seem to want to follow their path. Engineers want to be near other engineers. CEOs want to be near other CEOs.

Sociologists call this effect *clustering*.

For decades, Richard Florida, best known for his book *The Rise of the Creative Class*, has been studying the impact that density has on creativity. In one study, he and a research team studied over 240 different metropolitan areas, and compared the density of creative workers to the number of patents—a reflection of the level of innovation. They found that as density increased, and creative people found themselves more tightly packed, the number of patents also went up. Florida explained to me how big this impact was: "Places with high degrees of creative density were six times more innovative than places with low levels of creative density." It wasn't simply about high numbers of creatives in one geographical area; to spur them to best innovate, you needed them right on top of one another.

The reason has to do with what academics call *knowledge spillover*. This is the process by which ideas are shared among people and institutions as they meet, network, and talk to one another. When an artist lets it drop to another artist that they have discovered a new technique, or a researcher mentions a new technology to an entrepreneur, the knowledge transfers—or spills—to another person in the network. In essence, the teaching process is ongoing and everlasting.

Density is useful not only for finding teachers and mentors, but also collaborators. Says Florida, "In a great urban area, there are lots of talented people competing and collaborating, combining and recombining, forming and reforming with one another. Out of that very Darwinian process, out of that Darwinian profit motive, you begin to get great successes."

For these spillovers to happen, face-to-face relationships are also critical. It's not enough for people to know each other. Close physical proximity means that you and I bump into each other at the corner coffee shop, or while we're waiting for the bus, which gives us ample opportunities for impromptu meetings.

To become members of this environment, we are willing to pay premium prices to live and work in places like SoMa. Sure, the architecture is unique, and there are some historic buildings. But the big driver is that the people we want to *learn* from live there.

Membership in a cluster like SoMa is essential to finding a master teacher.

Now, it goes without saying that not everyone can afford to move to one of these dense, overpriced areas. But visiting, commuting, or spending as much time as you can there is essential to accessing the teachers who can accelerate creative success.

Once you find yourself there, the mechanism for finding teachers is straightforward: curiosity. Be like Wallach and ask questions; make it clear you *want* to learn. Successful people tend to admire this quality, and will be more willing to take you under their wing. If you're already experienced, find people who know something specific that you don't know and ask them questions. Kevin Ryan may have created billions of dollars in value, but he still aims to speak only 30 percent of the time in a meeting.

If you do this, you increase the odds of finding one or more master teachers, the first of the four necessary members of your creative community. These teachers will show you the patterns and formulas of your field so you don't have to start from scratch. They will also give you the feedback you need to master your craft more quickly, just as Max Martin did with his team of protégés.

The science of deliberate practice suggests that we all need to learn from someone more advanced than we are. But it's not enough to just *learn* the craft; eventually we also have to *create* something. The next member of your creative community is essential for executing your ideas.

Conflicting Collaborators

Brenda Chapman's mother drew a line on a piece of paper. Actually, it might better be described as a scribble.

She turned to four-year-old Brenda and asked her to make something out of it. Could Brenda learn to see things for more than what they appeared to be?

The little girl gazed down at the scribble and began connecting lines. She added a nose. She added ears (well, an approximation of ears). She drew a smile.

The girl paused, and looked at her work.

"It's a dog!"

It didn't look like a dog, but her mother beamed anyway. Brenda was being creative; she was making *something* out of *nothing*.

Before long, these games sparked a passion in Brenda Chapman. She would race home after school to draw and to watch hour after hour of Bugs Bunny cartoons. Wherever she was, she would be illustrating little scenes and characters. In Illinois, both the winters and the rainy seasons were long, and when cabin fever hit, Brenda, with the assistance of a large blanket, would transform the coffee table in her family's living room into a fort. She snuck under it, lay on her back, and started drawing on the underside of the table.

Her mother never caught her drawing on the family furniture (only when the family moved did Brenda's mother notice the figures drawn on the wood), but even if she had, she wouldn't have been upset. The important thing was that her daughter was pursuing her passions.

Soon Brenda announced that she wanted to become an animator. All those cartoons she watched after school, and all those sketches she made, became her new calling. In a blink, she was attending California Institute of the Arts and plotting her way into a career in animation.

Her mother didn't know it, but for Brenda Chapman those early illustration games would turn into a record-breaking animation career. Brenda would become the head of story for *The Lion King* (the first woman to hold a head of story role in a major studio animated film), and from there go on to codirect Dreamworks's *The Prince of Egypt*, becoming the first woman to direct a major studio animated film. She later shattered another glass ceiling as a writer and director of Disney-Pixar's *Brave*, becoming the first female winner of the Academy Award for Best Animated Feature.

Creating worlds is where Brenda Chapman feels most comfortable. As we spoke via videoconference, one thing she made clear to me is that creating a movie is about as far as you can get from a solo process. In fact, as far as Brenda is concerned, part of what makes a successful movie *is* the collaboration of multiple talented voices. Animated movies require story artists, animators, producers, screenwriters, directors, studio executives, and, of course, marketers. The process is iterative, and everyone gives one another feedback. These distinct voices working together allows for the broadest possible perspective on what movie audiences will enjoy.

Story artists, for example, draw a series of select frames and create a crucial comic-book version of the movie long before the animation team starts working. According to Chapman, this allows the director "to discover the characters and who they are and how they behave and what their emotional arc is. And is this story working? Are the themes right? Is the pacing right? It's really the preliminary blueprint, and the story artists are writing and acting and drawing at the same time."

Yes, Chapman was the director, but she still has gaps in her skills and knowledge. After all, Chapman is a story artist turned director, not an audio engineer or a marketer. Without other people around to execute those responsibilities, she wouldn't be able to accomplish her directorial and creative vision.

In most creative work, then, collaborators are essential. While this may seem obvious, when I interviewed creators, what surprised me was what *type* of collaborators were most effective. To unravel this, I talked to two young creatives who, it just so happened, were having an excellent year.

Stop, Collaborate, and Listen

Benj Pasek is exuberant, to the point where over the phone he sounds as though he is bouncing up and down. By contrast, Justin Paul is quiet, thoughtful, and prone to pausing before answering a question. Though potentially inharmonious, together the two form the aptly named and highly successful songwriting duo Pasek and Paul. They wrote the lyrics for 2017's hit movie *La La Land*, winning a Golden Globe and Academy Award for their efforts. Two weeks before I interviewed them, they won a Tony Award for their musical *Dear Evan Hansen*, which has become the permanently-sold-out-please-help-me-find-tickets Broadway show of the year.

The two became friends in college ballet class, sharing a common trait: a complete lack of coordination. As Pasek recalls, "We hid behind each other in class and figured out distractions so the teacher wouldn't pay attention to us." When Pasek and Paul first met, Pasek realized that Paul was a great piano player, and recruited him to help fix some pop songs Pasek had written in high school.

Soon, they began spending hours inside a tiny practice room on campus. Something clicked, and as Paul recalls, "Before we knew it we were writing songs together."

The following year, they both tried and failed to land leading parts in the school musical. Pasek was cast as the "man with camera" and Paul as "coroner/back-up dancer." Frustrated, they decided to create their own show, *Edges*, a collection of songs about finding meaning in your life. The rest of the cast consisted of the students who hadn't landed leading roles in the official school musical.

Edges wasn't just a means of killing time. A video version of the performance posted on Facebook went viral, and soon school groups around the country were requesting permission to perform *Edges*.

As a result, the duo quickly came to be seen as the future of musical theater. Celebrated producers wanted to mentor them. The press adored them. Still, what was it that Pasek and Paul saw in each other? What made their partnership work?

For Benj, Justin Paul provided the structure he needed to channel his ideas into a finished product. "Justin is very rigorous in his approach to his creative process, his approach to how he lives his life, and how he likes to organize time." To Pasek, this sort of systematic thinking is invaluable. "Without him, I wouldn't put as much importance on it. And I have learned how valuable that is to be able to create that kind of structure for one's self and for a creative process."

For his part, Pasek, the big thinker-dreamer-wanderer, needed

Paul, the planner-tinkerer-homebody. The process of creating a musical is seldom straightforward, and the Pasek-Paul dynamic and partnership allowed them both to flourish. Often, early productions take place outside of New York. If they do well in a secondary market, only then might they move Off-Broadway. *Dear Evan Hansen* began its life in a theater in Washington, D.C. The local press gave it rave reviews, but there was one problem: The final song of the first act didn't leave the audience with a feeling of dramatic tension. Worse, the song, "A Part of Me," wasn't exactly optimistic and some even deemed it judgmental. For the Off-Broadway production, Pasek and Paul auditioned a new song, "Surrounded." But that one didn't work, either.

Paul wanted to create something better, but how? He was stuck. That's when he called on Pasek, who began brainstorming, covering three pages of a journal with phrases. For Paul, this deluge of ideas was exactly what he needed. "Whether it's a bunch of great ideas or nine bad ideas and one great idea, it's helpful to just start the ideas flowing. Just to get things out there and start the process. Sometimes I get so paralyzed in seeing all the problems." From experience Paul knows that his preoccupation with process can land him in a rut. He needs a collaborator who can spark new ideas. Without Pasek, Paul tells me, "I'm prone to submit to being creatively stumped."

In the journal, one phrase caught Paul's eye: "You will be found." That phrase ended up as the title of *Dear Evan Hansen's* Act I final song. What's more, says Pasek, "It became a really big theme throughout the entire show of how do we save ourselves and how do we believe that we'll be okay." When *Dear Evan Hansen* premiered on Broadway, one line in *The New York Times* review felt especially sweet: "Particularly memorable is the soaring anthem that closes the first act, and is reprised in the second, 'You Will Be Found.'"

By providing the other with something that person can't do alone, Pasek and Paul have achieved outsize, and ongoing, success.

Having said that, collaboration is rarely all bliss. Sometimes the two men's differing perspectives cause friction. But rather than ending in compromise, or a weakened, muddled outcome, Paul believes their dueling perspectives make things *better* than if either one of them were working alone. "It's not just meeting in the middle, it's pushing forward so that instead of just moving on that horizontal plane, we're moving vertically as well."

For this reason, I call the ideal person to work with a *conflicting collaborator*. Basically, you don't want to collaborate with someone who is so easy to get along with that they don't push you. The goal is to find a person who will help you discover and overcome your flaws.

Ideal collaborators balance out each other's weaknesses and provide different perspectives. Creativity, after all, is a team sport, and even if you lack a close working partner like Benj Pasek or Justin Paul, other collaborators are out there. Pasek and Paul, for example, worked with a writer who wrote the dialogue for *Dear Evan Hansen*, as well as with a director, a producer who secured financing, not to mention a stellar cast of actors and singers.

In talent-dense environments, it's a lot easier to find a conflicting collaborator. For Benj Pasek and Justin Paul that environment was a college with a strong theater program. For Brenda Chapman, it was Cal Arts in Los Angeles. Many of the romance writers I spoke with found collaborators through a group called the Romance Writers of America, who offered not only friendship but also feedback and editing help.

The Internet, of course, has made collaboration and finding your tribe a lot more convenient. Online, the painter Jonathan Hardesty got suggestions and advice from his followers on a message board. Other creative people find collaborators *extremely* close to home. When Brenda Chapman launched her new production company, her partner was a talented former Disney animator, Kevin Lima, who also happened to be her husband.

Having a master teacher and a conflicting collaborator might seem to cover a lot of ground, but that doesn't mean your creative community is now complete. There are two other community members you need. One is a *modern muse*—an individual or a group of people who continually inspire and motivate you. If you devote your life to a creative profession, inevitably you will hit a few lows. Finding a support system that gets you through these rough spots will restore your energy and optimism, and make you that much more likely to achieve world-class success. Moreover, these muses often provide material and the raw ingredients of creativity. Best of all, they don't have to be purely supportive, either. In fact, as we'll see, sometimes the best inspiration comes from friendly competition.

A Modern Muse

For some kids, *Saturday Night Live* was simply a show that their parents watched. It was for "adults." But for Hari Kondabolu, *Saturday Night Live* was a childhood ritual, which isn't surprising, as he and his friends were obsessed with comedy. "We studied it without really studying it. We didn't know we were studying it, but we were watching *SNL*, taping it, rewatching it, watching Conan, taping it, rewatching it, watching stand-ups, listening to stand-up."

This relentless consumption led Kondabolu to a love and deep understanding of stand-up. Eventually, he combined his love of comedy with an equally deep passion for social justice to produce a unique form of social comedy. Today, *The New York Times* calls him "one of the most exciting political comics in stand-up today." He tours nationally, and his last album, *Mainstream American Comic*, debuted at number two on the Billboard Comedy Album chart.

I got in touch with him because I wanted to understand the creative process of comedians. As Kondabolu walked me through the process of writing a set, I was struck by how much of his success came from the community he'd built around himself.

It began when Kondabolu was young. His brother also loved comedy, and together the two were each other's early audiences. As Kondabolu got older, he discovered that his friends were a critical part of his career, as well. "Sometimes I have a funny conversation with friends, and most people when they have funny conversations with friends move on with their lives. I write them down, because that's what I do. I collect thoughts. I don't let anything go because it can be useful later." Kondabolu's friends aren't collaborators, per se, yet they serve as a powerful source of inspiration. Instead, they are examples of what I call *modern muses*: people who provide material for a creator to use as well as practical motivation. For him, other comedians also serve this role. Kondabolu has found that when he spends time with other comedians, his passion increases. "When comedians hang out together, they have a certain energy around them."

The creative life is full of emotional bumps, though maybe a better word is potholes. Creative people need to have others who supply them with the energy to power through those moments. Support and inspiration are always great, but the best modern muses also push through friendly competition.

Competing for Views

Casey Neistat is the original viral video star. Before YouTube even existed, he was creating short videos and uploading them online. In 2003, Neistat uploaded a three-minute film about his misadventures in trying to get Apple to replace his iPod's battery. Soon the video was picked up by the mainstream media, and Neistat's short video was seen by millions of viewers. HBO asked him to create his own show with similar content, but it lasted only one season. Feeling the brunt of mainstream rejection, Neistat went fully online, or as he puts it, "I ran to the welcoming open arms of YouTube." He posted his first videos about his life on the site in 2010 and today has over 8.9 million subscribers, with most of his videos garnering well over 1 million views, and some getting as many as 20 million. Along the way, Neistat also launched a video-sharing start-up, Beme, that was acquired by CNN for a reported $25 million.

Neistat may be the main star of his videos, but he is surrounded in life by countless creatively ambitious people.

"All of my friends have a career that is largely defined by their own creativity," Neistat tells me. This category also includes his wife, who founded and runs two jewelry companies. Being surrounded by creative energy doesn't merely motivate Neistat; it also elevates him and those around him: "We all thrive on one another, and it's a wonderfully beneficial relationship."

Most creators *like* having friends with whom they engage in friendly competition. YouTube star Connor Franta explains it well. "Every time one of my friends or one of my fellow YouTubers does something interesting and unique and next level, it's so inspiring to me. It makes me more thrilled to push myself and to try to get to that level."

Franta, like Neistat, has a desire shared by many creative artists: to meet other people who have the same ambition. "I try and surround myself with people who are doing really interesting, creative things. I have friends who have number-one bestselling albums on the iTunes charts. I have a friend who has had a line in Aéropostale that has made $100 million. I have a friend that's won a Teen Choice Award."

Surrounding yourself with other creative people, no matter their field, gives many creators the motivational boost they need to move through the lowest points of their work. The modern muse within your creative community doesn't simply inspire you via reassurance and validation; this person can also show you what is possible. For example, Connor Franta's friends demonstrated that YouTube stars don't have to stay within the lane of creating video, which paved the way for him to launch his future companies.

Identifying these people can be easy if they're already your friends. But what if you don't have friends like these? What if you are starting from scratch? To answer this, we'll revisit a colorful time in art history.

The Surprising Power of Renting a Loft

Jeremy Deller is a well-known artist who in 2004 was awarded the prestigious Turner Prize, which recognizes important but controversial modern art. Once upon a time, however, Deller was a twenty-year-old living in London with a recent art history degree and a fascination with Andy Warhol. Decades before the selfie generation, when Deller heard that Warhol was visiting London, he knew he had to get a picture with him.

Deller arrived at the Anthony d'Offay Gallery and there was Warhol, sitting at a table, signing mementos. Deller approached Warhol, and the artist scribbled his signature on Deller's baseball cap.

Afterward, as he paced around the gallery, Deller made conversation with a man who turned out to be a friend of Warhol's. Deller ended up getting invited to join Warhol and his group later for a drink.

When Deller arrived, Warhol and five of his friends were sitting around watching a comedian on a muted television set while listening to British glam rock. As drinks continued to pour through the night, Deller eventually became Warhol's artistic subject, agreeing to wear absurd hats and have his picture taken.

At the end of the night, Jeremy had gotten an invitation to spend two weeks at the Factory, Warhol's New York City studio, which also served as the gathering place for Warhol's social network.

Jeremy once described the Factory as an early version of today's start-up offices. "It was a very cool, funky, work/play environment, which is now de rigueur for tech companies like Google," he said.

"There were all these interconnecting rooms ... with a door that went into another building behind that was the headquarters of *Interview* [Warhol's magazine]. So the whole studio set-up was like being in Warhol's mind: You had the publishing section, filmmaking on the top, a painting studio, a business part, a dining room. He'd created a world."

What struck Jeremy was how social the iconic Warhol was at the Factory. "He was very chatty. It was intelligence gathering for him. He was always into networks, gossip. And then he would process it all into art." Deller described how Warhol "surrounded himself with people with different skills who had ambition and creativity. The working environment he created at the Factory is a norm now for creative people. There's a flow of people from whom you get ideas that feed into the art."

Warhol had built a community of modern muses and collaborators who seemingly shared his imagination and sensibility. While most of us count as our friends those people with whom we share common past experiences (college; our hometown), creative artists seek out individuals who are like-minded in their passion for innovation.

But you don't have to be an Andy Warhol to create this type of community.

Mihaly Csikszentmihalyi, the famous sociologist I wrote about earlier, continued to follow the careers of the art students from his research. At one point, he wrote of an unusual pattern among the ones who became successful. "Most of the young artists we studied who met with success after graduation started their careers in a loft. The six with the highest success had all rented lofts even before they left school. So far none of the unsuccessful former students did this."

Why would this be? Sure, a loft is a great way to store canvasses. But these massive spaces serve another purpose: It is a place where artists can surround themselves with collaborators, muses, and customers.

Csikszentmihalyi also found that lofts serve as a signal to the art world, communicating that the artist or artists who live there are serious and interested in public recognition.

In fact, one of the most *essential* roles of a successful loft is as a party space. Csikszentmihalyi writes, "A loft is an informal institution artists use to get in touch with the public. A loft without parties, without visitors, a loft that is not known in artistic circles, is not a loft in this institutional sense."

While most of us can't afford to build a giant office studio complex like Warhol, renting an artist's loft is an example of a lower-cost way you can attract the necessary members of a creative community, such as modern muses. Lofts even enable artists to find the fourth and final member of a creative community: a *prominent promoter*.

A Prominent Promoter

Maria Goeppert Mayer won the Nobel Prize in Physics (only the second woman after Marie Curie), joined the Manhattan Project in World War II, and over the course of her esteemed career published countless papers.

Today she's remembered as an academic great. Yet in 1931, at age twenty-six, she was an unknown young researcher.

How did she end up being awarded science's greatest prize?

Researcher Harriet Zuckerman was fascinated by her story and those of other Nobel laureates. Zuckerman wanted to know what we could learn from the early careers of these award winners: Were there clear steps that led to future success?

To answer this question, Zuckerman interviewed nearly every living American Nobel laureate in science. The book that reproduced her findings, *Scientific Elite: Nobel Laureates in the United States*, has become one of the primary texts in the study of "greatness."

One thing Zuckerman found was that future Nobel laureates were 170 percent more productive during their twenties than the typical academic. The average Nobel laureate she studied authored 7.9 papers in his or her twenties, in contrast to ordinary scientists, who were credited with only 2.9. You might well be thinking, *But of course! Wouldn't we expect them to be smarter, and harder-working? After all, that's why they ended up winning the Nobel Prize!* The thing is, when Zuckerman interviewed the laureates, she uncovered a different answer.

In 1931, Maria Goeppert Mayer was spending the summer working with the famed physicist Max Born, who would be awarded a Nobel himself in 1954. Together the two of them authored a paper entitled "Dynamic Lattice Theory of Crystals." Senior researchers often work with younger scientists, so that part comes as no surprise, but here is where the story took an unusual turn. Often, top researchers endeavor to keep the names of younger scientists off the final paper. For younger colleagues, it's considered part of "paying your dues." But most future Nobel laureates told Harriet Zuckerman that their mentors did the exact opposite—they not only shared credit, they often gave the younger scholars *more* credit. As Zuckerman writes, "Eminent masters exercised noblesse oblige not only by lengthening the bibliographies of their young associates (granting them joint authorship) but often by heightening the visibility of the junior contributions to the research in arranging to have their names appear first in the list of authors." In some cases, the master would even take their own name off the paper, leaving sole credit to the mentee.

It turns out it wasn't that the laureates were truly twice as productive as other academics, but rather that they worked for mentors who tended to share credit. This led to what is commonly called a "cumulative advantage," which is simply the idea that early advantages compound and can lead to large differences over time. By the time they reached their thirties, these young academics were better-known than other researchers, making it much harder for those researchers to catch up.

These future laureates had been boosted by others who were already credible. Senior researchers gave them clout and a foundation with which to build an advantage.

In previous chapters, I wrote that to be considered a "genius" you also need to be *recognized*. It's not enough to work hard, or to create technically competent work—you also need social acknowledgment that you're credible. For this reason especially, the last essential member of your creative community is a prominent promoter: someone with credibility who is willing to advocate for you and your work.

This phenomenon extends far beyond science. For example, prominent promoters are often seen in the music industry. The most obvious example is how more popular acts will bring lesser-known acts on tour with them as openers. In 2006, the country band Rascal Flatts booked a teenager named Taylor Swift to open for the last nine shows of their tour, helping to propel her to country music fame. By 2015, Taylor Swift was returning the favor, hiring the then-sixteen-year-old Shawn Mendes to open for her on her world tour.

Finding a prominent promoter may sound difficult—why would someone want to lend their credibility to you?—but studies tell us that not only do mentees benefit from these relationships, but promoters do, too.

Is It Better to Be an Insider or an Outsider?

Researchers at New York University wanted to understand the elements that make for an ideal team. Is it better to fill a team with skilled novices armed with "new" and "fresh" ideas, or established players who can lend experience and credibility to a project?

To learn the answer, they studied the film credits of 2,137 movies distributed by the major Hollywood movie studios between the years 1992 and 2003. For each of these films, they looked at seven critical crewmembers—producer, director, writer, editor, cinematographer, production designer, and composer—ultimately ending up with a list of 11,974 people. Next, using an online film industry database, they created maps of the professional networks of these same crewmembers.

Last, in hopes of judging how creatively successful the movies were, they looked at the number of major awards that each film won.

The research team wanted to find out if it's better to be an establishment figure (a prominent promoter) or a member of the undiscovered (who needs to be promoted). The answer, it turned out, was neither.

The best possible placement, the researchers concluded, was to be somewhere in the middle, that is to say, between the establishment and the fringe. The researchers found that by hugging the center, individuals "can benefit from being directly exposed to sources of social legitimacy." At the same time, partial membership in the fringe gives them ongoing access to novel ideas. "By not losing touch with the periphery, they can access fresh new inputs that are more likely to blossom on the fringe of the network while escaping the conformity pressures that are typical of a more socially entrenched field."

Being in the middle, between the establishment and the fringe, helps a person create content that is familiar and credible, but also novel.

Now what if you're successful already, and a member of the establishment? Alternatively, what if you're a true up-and-comer?

The NYU team produced a second conclusion: *Teams* containing both established and up-and-coming people gain the same advantage as a person who leans to the middle. This is because the people on the fringe give the establishment figures fresh ideas, and the establishment figures provide the necessary reputation and credibility. If you are already successful, this finding underscores how important it is for you to bring new and fresh voices onto your teams if you want to maximize your creative success. You need that source of novel ideas. And if you are an up-and-comer, you need a prominent promoter for recognition.

What's the best way to find one?

Unfortunately, this is one of those questions whose answer you may not like. Because in many cases, you *must* move. If you want to be in the film, TV, or music industry, you probably have to relocate to Los Angeles. If you want to be a modern or fine artist, at some point you probably have to head to New York.

If you're an established figure who already lives in one of those cities, don't forget that by lending your credibility to a newcomer, you not only pay it forward, you also gain from the other person's fresh ideas.

The Creative Community

When we glimpse a famous entrepreneur, actor, musician, or poet on the cover of a magazine, it can be easy to subscribe once again to the lone genius theory of creativity. Yet pretty much all the high-achieving creatives I spoke with for this book had built a creative community made up of a group of people who continue to help them on their journey toward creating hits.

These creative communities feature four types of individuals:

1. A Master Teacher—This is the person who teaches you the patterns and formulas of your craft or industry, to ensure that you create things with the right level of familiarity, while also giving you the feedback you need to hone your craft through deliberate practice.
2. A Conflicting Collaborator—Everyone has flaws. In order to make them nonfatal, you need to find a person or a group of individuals whose traits compensate for your flaws.
3. A Modern Muse—A life of creativity often involves getting your soul slapped around. You need to surround yourself with people who will motivate and inspire you to persevere, who can be a source of fresh ideas and even friendly competition to push you toward achieving your very best work.
4. A Prominent Promoter—To be a creative success, you need to be recognized as one. A prominent promoter already has credibility and is willing to share it with you. Not only does this benefit you, it also benefits the prominent promoter, who now has access to fresh ideas that help keep them at the right point on the creative curve.

The best innovators know that creative success isn't a solo adventure, and also know that a single key partner is insufficient. We all need in our orbits a community of people who will fill a variety of roles.

An Important Aside

Unfortunately, the importance of the creative community also makes it harder for women and minorities to find recognition in creative fields. In all my research, the lists of "top" entrepreneurs, artists, chiefs, and other creative people were dominated by white men. One study done by USC's Annenberg School for Communication found that of 414 major Hollywood studio productions, 85 percent of directors and 71 percent of screenwriters were male, and 87 percent of directors were white. Clearly, something is wrong.

One response to this inequity is the Black List, a media company named in a reference to the Hollywood screenwriters of the McCarthy era, many of whom were blacklisted as suspected Communists and therefore unable to find work. The company has two main services.

They started in 2005 with the creation of an annual list of the industry's best unproduced screenplays. The list is based on surveys of Hollywood executives. To date, more than three hundred of the scripts on the Black List have been turned into feature films, including *Slumdog Millionaire*, *The King's Speech*, and *Spotlight*, which in turn have generated over $26 billion in box office revenue.

In addition, the Black List now has a website where screenwriters can submit their screenplays, which in turn are rated by professional reviewers. When screenwriters submit a script they can choose to add their race and gender. The site's professional reviewers aren't privy to this data, but the Black List also publishes a report that compares the screenwriters' races and genders with the ratings their scripts received. The data found no meaningful difference in script ratings based on either race or gender. In fact, female writers actually scored slightly *higher* than their male counterparts did. Yet, as I mentioned, the industry is dominated by white men.

Clearly something structural prevents diverse voices from

breaking through in creative fields in the way they should. My guess is it has to do with an absence of a creative community. In a world where people seek out those who look, talk, and think like them, it can be a tough climb for women and minorities to find enough people to fill out their own creative communities.

Still, there's hope. The combination of awareness and tools like the Black List are creating progress. Says Franklin Leonard, who founded the website, "The Black List tries to contribute to this change both by expanding the pipeline of female writers and writers of color and by providing a meritocratic system of discovery." Of course, Leonard adds, there are also capitalist reasons for change. "Change is happening, driven largely by the dawning realization that producing films from and by women and people of color is, and always has been, great for business."

As you build your own creative community, remember that surrounding yourself with a diverse set of people not only enhances society, but also enhances your own creativity.

I've talked about the myths that have permeated creativity stories, the science of the creative curve, and three of the laws for mastering the creative curve. To explain the final law, I want to take you into the flavor lab of one of the world's most beloved and delectable brands.

Law IV: Iterations

'm sitting in a conference room named Chubby Hubby, at the world headquarters of Ben & Jerry's in Burlington, Vermont, a room that like many of the conference rooms here is named after one of the company's best-known ice cream flavors. My trip to this quirky state had so far lived up to my expectations. The gift shop at the hotel where I was staying sold both Ben & Jerry's ice cream and Vermont maple syrup. I saw electric cars everywhere on the city streets. In Ben & Jerry's parking lot there was even a Ben & Jerry's–branded Tesla.

The office was designed back in 1996, yet it has the feel of a Silicon Valley start-up. Long before Google and Facebook, Ben & Jerry's built an iconoclastic culture. Dogs are welcome in the office (my visit was punctuated by periodic barks), and a massive red slide by the main entrance transports employees from the second-floor conference room down to the first. In addition, there's a huge gym (which helps to counteract the "Ben 10"), a yoga room, and a private nursing room named the Milky Way.

I'd come to Vermont to spend the day observing the Ben & Jerry's creative process. I grew up in a household where their ice cream was more than just a dessert; for my mother, after a long day at work, it was therapy, a way to unwind.

As I made my way around the building, I couldn't help noticing empty pints of ice cream on every desk. Employees collected the flavors they worked on as a sort of cardboard trophy wall. Ben & Jerry's has had so many flavors that I assumed the process for creating a new one was by now efficient and direct: A food scientist would come up with a flavor idea, churn up a batch of the concoction, sample it, then supply an all-important verdict of "thumbs up" or "thumbs down." There would assuredly be consultation with other teams, but otherwise the process would be straightforward: begin with a delicious ice cream base, add some cookies, throw in some caramel, and voilà!, another new flavor takes its place on the Ben & Jerry's roster.

Instead, I found out that making new ice cream is serious business at Ben & Jerry's. I spent all day learning the four steps that Ben & Jerry's uses to create the ideal new flavor. And as we'll discuss, I couldn't help but realize that this same process is used not just for making ice cream but for other types of creative endeavors I witnessed.

The company's first store, which the founders opened in 1978, was a retrofitted gas station in Burlington. Jerry Greenfield (the "Jerry" of Ben & Jerry's) explained to me that in many ways the venture was born of necessity: "Ben and I started the ice cream shop because we wanted to work together, do something fun, because we always liked to eat, and because we were failing at the other things we were trying to do." They had taken a $5 remote education class in how to make ice cream and, armed with their newfound expertise, they decided to open up shop.

In no time at all they were a local phenomenon.

Today the company founded by two Burlington hippies is known around the world for its decadently rich flavors, including Chunky Monkey (my mother's favorite), Cherry Garcia, and Phish Food. Jerry's all-time favorite is the now-discontinued Coconut Almond Fudge Chip. He recalled, "It was like a trip to a tropical beach for the mind and taste buds." But what I wanted to know was how the brand comes up with their flavors and, while we're on the subject, *who* comes up with them?

Every year, Ben & Jerry's launches six to twelve new flavors. This means they are under continual pressure to create new products that land at the right point of the creative curve. But how had they operationalized this within their business? It turns out they have devised a repeatable system for achieving the vaunted sweet spot (pun very much intended) of familiarity and novelty.

When I probed more deeply, I was introduced to a few individuals who may have the best job in America: the Ben & Jerry's Flavor Gurus.

Ice Cream Tears

I was sitting in the "flavor lab" in the Ben & Jerry's headquarters, with tears running down my face.

These were not tears of joy or sadness.

The flavor lab was packed with "Flavor Gurus," Ben & Jerry's term for the food scientists and chefs whose job it is to create new ice cream flavors. In their civilian lives, all the gurus are serious foodies. Some are former restaurant chefs, others are chemists, yet they all have a pronounced knack for creating flavors. And at this moment, one Flavor Guru, Natalia, was using the lab's stove to prepare a spicy lunch that looked delectable, but was murder on my eyes.

Wiping away my tears, I asked the team to walk me through the process of how they create new ice cream flavors. My fantasy was that the group spent all day and night experimenting with and eating tons of ice cream, as they waited for a perfect combination of tastes and textures to click. Even though it's true that lots of ice cream is eaten in the lab (including by me), the actual process for creating flavors is complex and highly scientific. There are numerous stakeholders, shocking amounts of data, and an implicit utilization of the creative curve.

One reason why the process is so methodical is that it takes a long time—eighteen to twenty-four months—to create a new flavor. This means that the Flavor Gurus not only have to get a handle on what consumers like today, but what they'll like two years from now.

I was able to identify four distinct steps in their process: conceptualization, reduction, curation, and feedback. I wasn't surprised to realize that this pattern also recurs across all kinds of creative fields.

During the first step, ideation, their goal is to come up with as many potential flavor ideas as possible.

As they assemble this list, they consume (sometimes literally) numerous sources on food trends in the search for ideas.

The team, for example, might embark on a "trend trek," which involves traveling to another city to experience not just its ice cream, but its food and drinking culture. While on the trip, a pack of Gurus will descend on a grocery store to observe what people are buying, or go inside restaurants to take note of the flavors people are eating, or take a seat at one bar after the next to find out what bartenders are mixing into the latest cocktails. As Flavor Guru Chris explains, "You get up in the morning and you start eating, and you eat all day. You keep eating, and at the end of the day you go to dinner, and you keep eating. You're just engulfing yourself in that food world."

Chris, who is surprisingly skinny for an ice cream creator thanks to a biking obsession, gives me an example from a trip to Portland a few years earlier. When the team wandered out of their hotel, they stumbled across a nearby bar that offered a big stock of infused gins. One gin in particular stuck out—blueberry lavender—and the Gurus were blown away by its flavor. They returned to Vermont, determined to re-create that flavor. Recalls Chris, "We asked our suppliers if they could replicate those flavor concepts or those flavor combinations, and it worked!" Less than two years later Ben & Jerry's released their own signature blueberry lavender ice cream as part of the company's Greek Yogurt line.

But ideas and inspiration don't just derive from travel. The team also uses the Internet as well as traditional magazines to uncover trends. Flavor Guru Eric, who is lovingly called "Angry Chef," checks Tasting Table, a website that publishes menus from new restaurants all across America. Sarah, a relatively new Flavor Guru, finds Instagram a useful tool for spotting trends that are populating social feeds, including giant milkshakes with all kinds of crazy toppings. For other Gurus, magazines like *Bon Appétit* or *Food & Wine* are essential reads.

This consumption allows the company to understand which ideas are on the early upswing of the creative curve.

The Gurus also have a lot of in-house support, including an

internal consumer insights team tasked with researching the latest trends. All year the insights team and the entire company share their ideas through an internal Facebook Group dubbed the "FlavorHood," where company employees can post interesting recipes, food concepts, and insights on what competitors are doing that captured their attention.

Last, but importantly, Ben & Jerry's solicit flavor ideas from its customers. The company has a full-time team staffing the phones in Vermont. When customers phone or e-mail in suggestions, those suggestions are tracked and handed over to the brand management team, which looks at anywhere from ten to twelve *thousand* ideas every year. Many of these customer-supplied ideas have become flavors. For example, my morning conference room was named after one of them, the pretzel-laden Chubby Hubby flavor, which came about when a Ben & Jerry's customer attempted to play a practical joke at work by adding pretzels to a Ben & Jerry's pint and giving it to a coworker, informing her it was the company's latest flavor. The coworker not only believed the story, she found it *delicious*.

All these sources of information allow the team to observe trends early in their life cycle, which is imperative given the company's nearly two-year-long innovation cycle. After all, if Ben & Jerry's dreamed up concepts—flavors—once they'd reached the point of cliché, those flavors would be out of date by the time they went to market.

In 2016, the company launched a nondairy ice cream using almond milk (all the lactose intolerant people can rejoice). A brand manager told me that the Gurus had observed a growing interest in almond milk years earlier, but only recently had it moved beyond its niche health food status into the mainstream, along with the dairy-disavowing paleo diet. Explains Eric, "We track things from infancy."

In short, the Ben & Jerry's Flavor Gurus, brand managers, and marketers do *not* trust their raw instincts. Instead, they recognize their goal is simple: to listen to their audience. It's a deceptively simple paradigm, but one that's easy for successful people to ignore as their confidence grows.

In their search for burgeoning trends, the Ben & Jerry's team benefits from a wide variety of input—and by ingesting data from a variety of sources, they're conducting their own form of consumption.

So once they have digested these trends, how do the Gurus come up with ideas worth trying? This next step is where constraints play a critical role.

Conceptualization

Ice cream is based on chemistry. As Eric told me, "If the ingredients are not in balance, then you don't get that smooth, creamy texture. Too much protein and it is chalky. Too much sugar solids and it doesn't freeze hard." Ben & Jerry's also has a policy that products must have fewer than 250 calories and under twenty-five grams of sugar per serving. These constraints create a familiar baseline for what Ben & Jerry's ice cream should taste like, allowing them to create the right amount of novelty.

What's more, since Ben & Jerry's is focused on (and their consumers have come to expect) social justice, the company's ingredients must be non-GMO sourced by origin, Fairtrade, and kosher-certified. As a result, the Gurus may only create flavors whose ingredients meet or surpass that high bar, meaning that the team is in contact with its suppliers year-round to understand what is available.

Ben & Jerry's also has manufacturing constraints to worry about. Breaking these constraints can have serious consequences.

If you've ever mixed chocolate with your movie theater popcorn, you already know how delicious that combination is, and the Ben & Jerry's team agreed. The gurus created the flavor in the lab with hopes of blockbuster flavor. Everybody loved the test batch. But when the company produced the first run and sent it out to stores, the customer service team was inundated with complaints: the popcorn had gotten soggy!

It seems that when popcorn spends weeks in transit going from the factory floor to freezer shelves and inside people's homes, it absorbs the innate moisture of the ice cream. In fact, just about anything that mixes with ice cream gets soft by the time it reaches a home freezer.

This softening phenomenon may have been bad for popcorn, but in other ways it is useful. In the lab, I was surprised to find that the cookie pieces Ben & Jerry's uses are crunchy (I may have had a "few"), yet when you eat one of Ben & Jerry's cookie-laden flavors, you'll notice the cookie pieces are soft. The moisture absorption may create a subpar experience with popcorn, but it works in cookies' favor, making them chewy and delicious.

The final constraint is shelf space. Ben & Jerry's has a limited variety of pints they can ship, and if they ship too many similar flavors, they run the risk of tiring out their audience. As Dena Wimette, a company R&D manager, told me, "A coffee flavor is never going to sell as well as a caramel flavor is, but how many caramel flavors do we need?"

Because of these constraints, the research team is able to brainstorm within a smaller universe of possibilities. They take their research, viewed through the lens of their constraints, and come up with a list of 200 flavor profiles, like "Vanilla ice cream with cherries and fudge flakes." This is what I call the *conceptualization* stage, where creatives generate a set of plausible ideas. The starting number of 200 is arbitrary, but it is important to come up with a wide range of reasonable options that can then be refined.

Reduction

Which brings us to the next step: editing 200 possibilities to around fifteen ideas that are actually worth testing.

Artists are traditionally reluctant to let others see their work before it is done. But great creatives—and great companies—know that the only way to consistently create in the sweet spot of the creative curve is by putting their work before an audience early and often. It is important to do this *before* investing in creation, narrowing your options to those that have a *reasonable probability* of success. From there, intuition and judgment usually govern the final choices.

How does Ben & Jerry's do this?

ChunkMail, the Ben & Jerry's e-mail newsletter, has over 700,000 subscribers, all devout fans of the product. Once the team has assembled the list of 200 flavor profiles, it sends a one-sentence description of these flavors to a representative section of the e-mail list as a survey, and asks two questions on a five-point scale for each flavor idea:

How likely are you to buy this flavor?
How unique is this flavor?

Basically, what the team wants to know is how familiar and novel the flavor choices are. (In effect, the team is trying to measure the core elements of the creative curve.) "How likely are you to buy this flavor?" asks respondents to compare a new possibility to the flavors they know and love already—which is another way of saying "familiarity." "I think if you look at what most people want, it's vanilla ice cream with brownies and caramel or chocolate ice cream flavors with cookies and caramel," Dena told me. "Those are always at the top, and we love to make ice creams with caramel and brownies." But the challenge for her and the other Gurus is to keep moving the brand forward by "doing things that are unique but are still interesting enough that people would want to buy them." That is why the question on uniqueness is critical. The goal isn't just finding things that consumers say they would buy, but also things that are novel and have a high enough purchase intent—things, that is to say, at the ideal place of the creative curve.

It's not an exact science, but data guides the team on how their audience perceives the proposed 200 flavors. This testing *matters*, too; every Guru said so. Think about it: If you spend all day dreaming about, working on, and tasting ice cream, you can't really call yourself an accurate representation of the true Ben & Jerry's customer. To understand how best to go forward, the Gurus need a ream of external input. The question isn't just whether a new flavor will *taste* good but, rather, will it sell enough pints?

From this testing, the team settles on the fifteen flavors they believe have the ideal balance of novelty and familiarity.

This is the *reduction* step. To create ideas that stick, you need to go from a wide-ranging list of plausible ideas to a data-driven subset of ideas that have strong consumer and audience indicators. Your goal is to constantly refine your understanding of where an idea will fall on the creative curve.

For many creatives, this early testing can be scary. After all, they risk criticism and rejection.

But it's also the only way to predict success.

After this data-driven approach, it's time for the third phase of the creative process: curation.

Curation

This is where the ice cream eating begins.

At this point, the Flavor Gurus figure out how to make small batches of the fifteen flavors on their list. As Chris explained to me, "Initially, it's more of a culinary development process. Sometimes that requires us to go to the local grocery store, buy produce, and make our own fillings whether it be jam or mint brownies, just to get that creativity flowing."

This aspect matters, because the human element matters. Notes one brand manager, "So far they've done well on paper, but we've got to make sure that they're actually going to taste good." After making small handmade batches of all fifteen flavors, the Gurus taste them and seek additional feedback from other teams and stakeholders. According to Chris, "We have a cutting room where we all come into the room and we'll have ten or fifteen pints that we're scooping through, we're serving, we're evaluating, we're tweaking, we're saying, 'This is disgusting,' and we throw it away or we just adapt from there."

Soon the Gurus will select all the flavors they like. If they can't make up their minds about a certain flavor, often they'll ship samples to longtime customers, or place tiny batches into their retail stores and see what fans think.

This is the *curation* process. It is when you rely on people, either internally or externally, to give you qualitative perspectives. While the surveying done in the reduction stage is useful for getting in the right ballpark, you need to gather deeper context to confirm data and intuition.

Once they're done curating their final flavors, they begin scaling up production. Six pints becomes six gallons, which turns into ten thousand gallons. But how do the people who work at Ben & Jerry's know whether they got it right?

Feedback

Have you ever had dill pickle ice cream?

At one point, as I was talking to the Flavor Gurus, they told me about a recent experiment where they created sorbet using dill pickle juice. "It's excellent!" one of them, Eric, exclaimed. My poker face broke, replaced by a somewhat shocked look, but before I could say anything, or protest, Eric turned to one of his colleagues. "Just pull it out. It'll temper fairly quickly."

This is how I ended up eating a few spoonfuls of pickle-flavored Ben & Jerry's.

The real surprise, though, was the taste.

Dill pickle sorbet is *delicious*. I don't mean that it's adequate, or okay, or "interesting." I mean it was go-back-for-second-and-thirds-*delicious*. My mouth is watering just writing about it.

So, when will we all see pickle flavors on freezer shelves?

As you may have guessed, the answer is probably never. As the team has learned, even phenomenal ideas need to be familiar enough to appeal to larger audiences. Kombuchas and fermented foods including pickles may be an emerging food trend, but it's not clear this trend is widespread enough to persuade the Gurus that it is ready to advance into the mainstream. As Chris explains, "It's a little tough because our development cycle is so long, so the trends that are really quick flashes in the pan, those are really hard for us to get unless we can see them coming way in advance, which is a challenge on its own. We try to get trends, if we see them, right before they start to spike up."

Since, among other things, the team is in the business of predicting what consumers will want in two years, post-launch feedback is obviously critical to their process. Despite months of planning, testing, and strategizing, their judgment can still be off, and their execution can still get messed up. This is the feedback stage, where creators can gauge if they were in the creative curve's sweet spot.

To do this, they need more data.

The earliest data arrives via phone calls, e-mails, and social media. Ben & Jerry's eventually receives sales data, but during the early stages, fan reactions, either positive or negative, matter the most. If for some reason they didn't nail a flavor, they need to figure out why: What faulty assumptions led to that failure? When you think about it, the goal of any creative process isn't just to create great results but also to improve the process itself. The processes themselves are a "product" that can be tweaked and enhanced. By improving these workflows, creative people not only come up with new ideas faster, they also have a higher likelihood of repeating their success.

And, because of the way that consumers change their preferences, as illustrated in the creative curve, ideas that worked once can lose their specialness. Creators need to measure and assess constantly. To this end, Chris tells me, "We caught the Greek yogurt trend at the right time, and that was a huge innovation for us, and now we're slowly getting rid of them." The Ben & Jerry's fan base is moving on to something else.

The life and death of flavors is an essential part of the creative process. Which is why toward the end of my trip, I found myself paying a visit to the Flavor Graveyard just up the hill from the factory. There, marked by surprisingly serious-looking tombstones made of Vermont marble, was a testament to all the flavors that have come and gone over the years (RIP blueberry lavender swirl).

The rise and fall of the creative curve brings ideas from nothingness to prominence, and back to nothingness again. And that's okay.

Creative iterations are critical to making great products of all types. That is why before even starting, creative people need to understand where their ideas will be on the bell curve of popularity. Across the various fields I studied, creative people all had their own methods of refining ideas in order to end up with a shortlist of those with the highest probability of success. While I don't have a cutesy acronym for this process, in every field creators used the four steps I outlined at Ben & Jerry's:

Conceptualization, Reduction, Curation, and Feedback.

This iteration process allows anyone to refine their work to find the ideal spot on the creative curve.

What does this look like in other fields? Is making ice cream truly the same as, say, making movies?

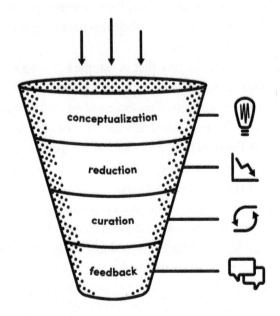

The Data of Film

One of the most surprising things I learned over the course of my research into creative success was how *similar* creative processes are across different fields. Writers had similar methods to entrepreneurs. Chefs planned things out the same way songwriters do. And movie producers create hit movies the same way that Ben & Jerry's launches new flavors.

All commercial creativity in the end is about the same thing: creating products that will match—and intersect with—an audience's taste at a particular point in time.

The creative process for making a movie, including the data that goes into crafting the final film, is an excellent example of listening to what an audience wants.

Nina Jacobson is one of the most influential people in Hollywood. She previously was the president of Walt Disney Motion Pictures, where she was responsible for shepherding countless hits into theaters, ranging from *Pirates of the Caribbean* to *The Sixth Sense*. Today she is the founder and CEO of Color Force, the production company responsible for the *Hunger Games* movie franchise that generated $3 billion worldwide. Jacobson and Color Force were also responsible for the award-winning *The People v. O. J. Simpson* TV series. When we spoke, Jacobson was in Malaysia filming a new movie called *Crazy Rich Asians*, based on the bestselling book of the same name that now has over one million copies in print.

Over a crackly cell phone connection, we started talking about how she ended up in Hollywood. Jacobson majored in semiotics at Brown University, and described the major as "a little Marxist theory, a little feminist theory, and a little psychoanalytic theory. It's very Brown," she added with a laugh.

In college, she also became enchanted by her classes in film theory. Here was a subject that, like semiotics, had infinite layers of complexity, and Jacobson loved it. "The idea of knowledge that was an endless spiral, and you could keep going deeper and deeper and you would never get to the end, you would never feel like you'd mastered it."

After graduation, she found her way west, where she soon landed a job as a script reader, reading two scripts a day and writing summaries to studio executives explaining whether or not a script was worth pursuing. Without knowing it, this was a period of focused consumption. "The more you read, the more you develop the language to articulate the feelings that the work provokes." In short, Jacobson was absorbing popular taste in the same way our former video store clerk turned Netflix head, Ted Sarandos, learned about movies back in Arizona.

Recognized for her hard work and keen insights, her career started to take off, and by the time she was thirty-six she had taken the helm of Walt Disney Motion Pictures Group. In 2007, she founded Color Force.

Intrigued by how films, and the film industry, use iterative processes and data, I called her to find out how studios try to craft the perfect blockbuster.

Screenwriting comes first. Jacobson explained that the process of screenwriting is far different from a writer sealing themselves up in a remote escape in the woods, emerging after they have typed the words "The End." Instead, the screenwriter, or, today, several screenwriters, works alongside the producer, the director, and sometimes even the cast. "In the early stages of a script, you may be trying out major changes," Jacobson says. "What if we got rid of this character entirely? What if we tried this structural approach?" Then as the big pieces become clear, you start to work on refining the smaller pieces. Are individual scenes working? Does a certain character need more lines?

Her goal? "How do I get every scene to fire on multiple cylinders, so that the character's advancing, the scene is advancing, and the story's advancing?" These iterations continue throughout the entire process; until you see the pieces come to life you can't really know whether or not a script will work, which is why Jacobson tries to engage everyone possible in the project. "I think listening is underrated in creativity," she adds.

For Jacobson, listening to the audience permeates the entire movie-making process. Even after the film is edited, test screenings can assess how audiences react. Says Jacobson, "If you want people to feel the things that you hope and aspire for them to feel, you want to have an opportunity to find out if they feel those things."

Understanding the audience—even experienced, renowned film industry veterans like Nina Jacobson recognize its importance. I decided that diving into the data behind Hollywood would be a good way to uncover how creatives can best use data in their work. For example, how do test screenings work? Where else has data become part of the film process?

Putting You in a Box

Traditionally, movie marketers divide film audiences into four quadrants: male, female, over twenty-five, and under twenty-five.

Film Demographic Quadrants

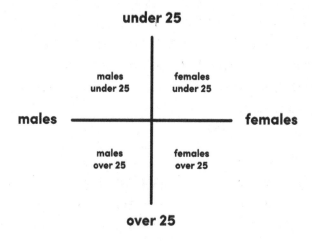

The overriding philosophy, if we can call it that, is that movies and movie marketing are ideally targeted to one or more of these four demographics. For example, a romantic comedy might be aimed at females both over and under twenty-five, whereas a tentpole blockbuster like *Avatar* can be marketed to all four quadrants.

Hollywood's quadrant approach was made popular by the National Research Group, a movie research company founded in 1978 by two former political pollsters who decided to apply their election-winning techniques to the box office. The two cofounders left in the early 2000s, but Jon Penn, the current CEO of National Research Group, explained to me the political analogy: "I think politics is about finding your base and identifying who your swing voter is. I think that's the same type of framework we bring to movie polling and research, which is 'Who's your base and who's your incremental swing, and what's the message that's going to work with both?'"

For a long time, the quadrant played a fundamental role in identifying these groups. Penn elaborates: "If you think of the quadrants, it's like a way to replicate how in politics you have Democrats, Republicans, and independents. It's creating a framework so that you can then use it as a lens to understand different demographic groups." Today, the quadrant has undergone a few modifications and is being replaced with more nuanced psychographic groups (environmentalist moms, image-focused male teenagers, etc.), but overall, the critical role of testing is very much a part of the movie business.

Hollywood executives use data in three main ways. First, will the target quadrant genuinely enjoy the movie in question? Second, do the trailers and ads appeal to the right group? Third, how does the public perceive the movie in the weeks before the opening weekend? Is the buzz good, bad, or neutral? In this way, they can modify their messaging and strategy if needed.

A Fatal Test

Janet walked out of the movie theater, looking and feeling bored, and tired (it had been a long week). She'd just sat through an early preview of *Fatal Attraction*, and like most of the test audience, she didn't love it.

The main reason? The ending was not satisfying. The movie tells the story of a mistress who becomes obsessed with her lover. In the original version, the mistress kills herself and frames her lover for her own murder. However, it left audiences feeling that the mistress didn't get her due punishment.

The studio executive knew they had a problem, but how would they fix it?

Fatal Attraction went on to be nominated for six Academy Awards and generated $320 million at the box office worldwide ($688 million in today's value). Having said that, the version of *Fatal Attraction* that reached those heights wasn't the same *Fatal Attraction* that early test audiences saw.

To get there, the studio had to reshoot the entire ending.

In the new ending, the wife, played by Anne Archer, shoots the one-time mistress, played by Glenn Close, in a riveting bathroom scene, ultimately creating the psychothriller ending that defined the film.

Previews, or, as the trade lingo calls them, "recruited audience screenings," have become an essential means of testing new releases. Jacobson explains: "Oftentimes it's easy to think, 'Oh, it's so extrinsic to the creative process to ask a bunch of consumers basically what they think,' but we're making movies for audiences, so it's actually very helpful to know what they think."

The movie research industry has evolved since the early days of the National Research Group. Kevin Goetz, the founder and CEO of Screen Engine/ASI, a leading Hollywood research firm, specializes in recruited audience screenings and over the years has conducted what he estimates are "well over ten thousand" previews. I spoke to him to better understand how these screenings worked, and whether those practices could be applied outside the movie industry.

Studios generally hold test screenings once there's a rough cut of a film. The music track or a few special effects may be missing, but for the most part the story and rhythm of the film are set. In the crowd are men and women who match the target audience, at least based on the preliminary marketing strategy.

Fearing that people might record the movie or tweet a spoiler, security is tight: viewers are asked to sign a confidentiality agreement, leave their phones outside the theater, and pass through metal detectors.

When the film ends, audience members fill out a survey card with questions on topics ranging from their favorite characters and scenes to whether the film moved too slowly or too quickly. The two most important questions are:

How likely are you to "definitely" recommend the movie?
How do you rate the movie overall?

The results of this, the quantitative part of the research, can often decide the fate of a film. Will portions of it need to be reshot? Is it worth all those precious marketing dollars?

Regarding these survey results, filmmakers and studio executives are looking for movies that score significantly above average. But it's not over yet. Next, a microcosm of the audience is selected to stay in their seats and participate in a discussion so that the studio can better understand the *why* behind the data. If you are unlikely to recommend the film, why? Is it because you hated the main character? Did you feel the plot dragged? "At a test screening, the focus group is often the intersection of art and science," says Goetz. "A creative moderator can tease out visceral responses that moviegoers wouldn't necessarily write about in their questionnaires." This mix of quantitative and qualitative data gives filmmakers and studio executives valuable insights into where the movie works, where it doesn't, and the best ways to fix it.

In Goetz's experience, most filmmakers and executives understand the power and value of testing. Rather than a tool designed to punish filmmakers, Goetz sees the data as a tool for refining audience reaction. "I'd like to think I approach it in a healthy way; I don't see it as some report card in order to beat people up. But when you're making a motion picture, you're making that picture for a large audience and, particularly when you're doing it for a studio, the stakes are extremely high and economic realities are undeniable."

Movies, in essence, are a creative endeavor among screenwriters, directors, and producers. But like any other creative project, the industry relies on iterations and data to refine their products in order to match what audiences want, while at the same time providing just enough novelty to intrigue them.

This data doesn't stop once the film is cut.

Movie marketers continue to rely heavily on data to optimize their campaigns to bring people into theaters. The techniques they use have a unique origin, too: the White House.

Presidential Data

It's 1996. President Bill Clinton is standing at the podium in front of the Democratic National Convention.

"So tonight, let us resolve to build that bridge to the twenty-first century, to meet our challenges and protect our values."

The theme of Clinton's speech was clear. The president and his team had decided he would focus on the values Clinton shared with every single American voter.

That word, *values*, popped up consistently throughout the speech. "If we want to build that bridge to the twenty-first century," Clinton thundered, "we have to be willing to say loud and clear: If you believe in the values of the Constitution, the Bill of Rights, the Declaration of Independence, if you're willing to work hard and play by the rules, you are part of our family. And we're proud to be with you."

That night, the president was acting upon the results of data collected by a pollster via nationwide phone and mall interviews (which are, in fact, interviews conducted in shopping malls). On edge after the 1994 midterm elections, in which the Democrats lost the House of Representatives, the president's team embarked on a practice of ruthlessly testing their message, choosing ads and even themes based on what voters best responded to in small testing rooms.

Clinton's poll-tested message worked. When Americans voted in 1996, Bill Clinton received 379 electoral votes to Bob Dole's 159. Presidents and politicians of both parties and at all levels have since used polling and testing to craft the perfect messages to win elections, gain approval from their constituents, and get bills passed.

Similar research helps guide movies to box office success. In the weeks before the opening of a movie, researchers test the trailers and TV ads we see.

National Research Group's Jon Penn explains the process: "You have a movie, and we try to distill the whole movie into its core essence and then try to identify what are the ten to twelve different big themes that really make your film compelling and unique? Those are the building blocks for the creative marketing campaign." The goal? To find a "good sense of your assets, your liabilities, your key characters, your story hooks, your tagline, so you can come up with a strategic blueprint before you get into testing the visual material."

Once the trailer is cut, does the testing stop? Hardly. In the old days, studios would show the trailers to selected mall audiences to gauge their feedback. They did this by using a "dial test." Viewers would twist a dial to the left or right depending on how much they liked or disliked certain segments of the trailer. The dial test is now often replaced by an online equivalent, the goal being to reach a larger, more representative audience.

What filmmakers and studio stakeholders are really after is maximizing the odds that undecided potential audience members—the equivalent of election swing voters—will buy tickets to the movie. Penn explained, "Trailer testing is an iterative process. You're going to go into the lab, if you will, which is talking to consumers either in person or online and you're going to try out different creative explorations of what you think is the most marketable premise to sell the movie." Along the way, testing uncovers key elements to which the audience responds. "You may change up the trailer, you might have different beginnings, you may have different endings. You may play with tone, you may play with music. If it's a comedy, making sure you have at least four or five key hilarious moments in the trailer, two or three in a TV spot."

The use of data doesn't stop here.

Twenty-four hours before Election Day, politicians are still polling for clues about how they'll fare when constituents finally vote. If they're not making the right progress, they use the data to tweak their strategy.

Film studios do the same thing.

It's known as "tracking."

If you think politicians face pressure, for film studios, every weekend is essentially Election Day. Which film will win the box office? In the hope of gaining a competitive advantage, movie researchers survey people nationwide to find out what movies they're most likely to watch. Nina Jacobson explains the process: "Tracking is when a market research firm will survey people randomly and say, 'What movies are coming out this weekend?'" In short, do people know your movie is coming out? This is what is called *unaided awareness*, and it represents how broadly the marketing has infiltrated the culture.

The polls address two additional critical questions. Jacobson explains: "Then you go, 'Hey, have you heard of *Hunger Games?*' 'Oh yeah, I've heard of that.' That's aided awareness." Lastly, the pollsters ask respondents if they plan on seeing the movie in question that weekend, which in turn allows movie executives to assess whether or not their ads worked or came up short.

Says Jacobson, "It is sometimes a very good indicator, and you get a sense of whether it's going to be a big opening or a weak opening." The data may not be precisely predictive, but it can alert filmmakers to potential problems, allowing them to refine or modify their strategies. If a movie is underperforming with a key quadrant, the studio can target a greater percentage of their remaining budget to try to solve the problem.

Politicians either win or lose an election, and movies have a similar end game: box office receipts. They are perhaps the ultimate feedback that validates and confirms the assumptions and systems filmmakers used through their iterations.

Across creative fields, data-driven iterations are critical to refining products and messages for the creative curve. In many industries, this requires the use of data, both to test audience response and to judge whether your effort was successful. By hitting the mark, most creative people gain confidence in their creative process. Miss the mark, and they know that somewhere along the line they made a faulty assumption.

If you're an independent creator, this can sound overwhelming. How can you use data if you can't afford expensive tools or technology?

To explore this, I talked to someone earlier in their creative career.

In the previous chapters, we talked to a handful of romance writers at the top of their field. This time around, I spoke with an "up-and-coming" writer who's managed to garner a measure of early success without the backing of a major publisher.

In part, she did this through the use of *free* data.

Another Side of Heidi

By day, Heidi Joy Tretheway works as a corporate marketer in charge of content marketing for tech companies, helping craft content to drive new business leads.

By night, Heidi writes what she calls "smart smut books."

Nestled in her Portland, Oregon, home, she stays up every night once her children are asleep, sits down at her computer, and starts typing.

Tretheway is a part of the cultural movement that's seen self-published romance authors like Kristen Ashley gain success through unconventional back channels.

Tretheway isn't embarrassed about what she does. "I write really dirty books and it's awesome."

Tretheway is a former customer of mine, and once as we were preparing to discuss digital marketing over lunch, she mentioned she was writing a book. I was soon peppering her with questions, and learning how her evening writing hobby has built her a growing fandom.

Tretheway, it turns out, is a popular e-book writer. Her most popular series, Tattoo Thief, has been downloaded on Amazon over 102,000 times.

Her writing career began inauspiciously. Her first novel, Won't Last Long, was downloaded only 125 times.

Though she doesn't outsell someone like Kristen Ashley, Tretheway has achieved a level of success that any part-time writer would envy. How did she go from 125 downloads to 102,000?

When her first book flopped, Tretheway was depressed. The book had taken her a decade to finish.

For her next book, she was determined to do things differently.

Rather than wait for a great idea to hit her, Tretheway began building a community of authors and studying story structure. One day, she had the idea of using a house sitter who was also a sexual voyeur as her protagonist. But instead of starting to write, she sat back and listened to what her author community had to say.

She quickly gleaned two things. The first was that new adult fiction, that is to say, books focusing on characters eighteen to thirty years old (instead of older characters) were starting to perform really well, and second, for some reason rock stars made especially popular protagonists at the time.

Which is why she decided to write her new novel about a young rock star and his voyeuristic house sitter. "I took my initial idea and fit it into a box that I knew was marketable. It turned out that actually made it *extremely* marketable. It took off better than it probably had any right to because it hit right in the right zone."

With over 100,000 downloads, Tretheway is now convinced that this kind of analysis is critical to marketing a book. Today she does this not only by talking to other writers but also by studying the Kindle sales charts, which allows her to get a strong sense of what's selling and what's relevant. "Right now, stepbrothers are very hot. It makes me kind of want to vomit, but there are so many successful books with these awkward love triangles."

Thanks to her creative community and free Amazon data, Tretheway can better understand what her reading audience cares about. What's more, she has used that data to do a lot more than select her genre and narrow down her characters.

Romance novels are often written as multipart series. People read the first book, and in the best-case scenario get hooked and read the rest of the series. It's a key part of the romance novel business model, to the point where many romance writers give away their first book for free online, hoping readers will find it so irresistible they'll buy all the others in the series.

For Tretheway, sequels represent an opportunity.

"Everybody will tell you don't ever read your reviews," but she decided to do it anyway. "What I learned was people did not like the fact that my main character was offstage for much of the book." She also discovered that readers disliked a second principal character.

Armed with this practical feedback, Tretheway was better able to serve her audience. In sequels, she improved the likability of the character in question, and wrote the new male protagonist into the book from the beginning. Then, to help ensure readers kept on with the series, she tacked on the first few chapters of the next book as a bonus section at the end of the first book.

The result?

The second book got markedly better reviews than the first.

Tretheway may not have been privy to "big data," but she was nonetheless able to use available public data to help her refine a market opportunity—while also improving the quality of her product.

The point I'm trying to make is that data doesn't have to be expensive or part of some fancy system to be useful. Simple data can be used in any creative field to help someone get better at what they are doing.

Painters can get online feedback.

Chefs can read their Yelp reviews.

Writers can see what topics are doing well on social media.

Sure, if you work in a large company, you typically have paid data sources, as well as the technology to access them. But even in big companies, many data techniques are decidedly low-tech. Ben & Jerry's, for example, sends e-mail surveys out to ice cream fans, which is something anyone can do using free online tools. What's more, many techniques historically used by large companies have now become accessible to small companies and individuals. Google Surveys, for one, allows anyone to assess a targeted group of users for as little as fifteen cents per response. For thirty dollars, you can assemble 200 people in a mini online focus group. Another service, PickFu, makes it easy to survey basic split-test questions in hours for as little as twenty dollars.

Again, any creative person can benefit from better understanding their target audience. Instead of seeing creativity as a series of eureka moments and sudden epiphanies, successful creatives who use data-driven iterations are far more likely to master the creative curve. Whether you're a writer, a movie studio, or an ice cream flavor guru, it pays to follow the data-driven steps and really, truly listen to your audience.

As I spoke with all kinds of creative people for this book, I was struck by how often their stories mirrored one another. Creative success does indeed have a pattern. The biggest secret to creating something your audience will love? *Listen to them.*

The use of data-driven processes to refine ideas is the fourth and last law of creativity.

By this point, you know the history of creativity, the driving forces behind trends, and the four steps you can take to maximize your odds of creating things that have a chance of going big and wide.

This is where I would *like* to leave you—I hope inspired and newly motivated that you can accomplish great artistic and entrepreneurial feats. But as I was writing this book, one thing kept worrying me. One concern that I need to convey before you embark on your next creative adventure.

Epilogue

t was 1990.

J. K. Rowling was stuck on the train from Manchester to London. The train was delayed, and it was looking less and less likely she'd reach London on time. Her mind started to wander.

Then, as she later told *The New York Times*, "It was the most incredible feeling . . . out of nowhere, it just fell from above."

Suddenly the ideas for the characters inhabiting a magical world began filling her brain, starting with Harry Potter. "I could see Harry very clearly; this scrawny little boy, and it was the most physical rush of excitement. I've never felt that excited about anything to do with writing. I've never had an idea that gave me such a physical response."

The mythology around the creation of Harry Potter would have us believe that Rowling then scribbled her ideas on a napkin. In truth, she had no paper with her. "I'm rummaging through this bag to try and find a pen or a pencil or anything. I didn't even have an eyeliner on me. So I just had to sit and think. And for four hours, because the train was delayed, I had all these ideas bubbling up through my head."

Rowling continued, "By the end of that train journey I knew it was going to be a seven-book series. I know that's extraordinarily arrogant for somebody who had never been published but that's how it came to me."

That night, in her apartment in the Clapham Junction neighborhood of London, she began writing things down in her notebook.

She never could have known that, by 2016, the Harry Potter series would have sold an estimated $7.7 billion of books, *plus* revenue from film versions, theme parks, exhibitions, a new play that debuted in London in 2016, and an ever-growing list of Harry Potter–themed products.

Like McCartney's "Yesterday," Harry Potter's spontaneous origin has become a legend for Rowling's fans, and throughout literature.

Rowling reinforces the notion of sudden insight. When pressed to explain where her ideas came from, she demurs. "I [have] no idea where ideas come from and I hope I never find [out]; it would spoil the excitement for me if it turned out I just have a funny little wrinkle on the surface of my brain which makes me think about invisible train platforms."

While this image of Rowling makes her a poster child for the inspiration theory of creativity, in truth Rowling is a near-perfect example of someone following the four laws of the creative curve.

Consumption and Constraints

As a child, Rowling was a rabid reader, consuming one novel after the next. Like many of the creative artists I profiled, she came of age in a rough home environment. Her mother's multiple sclerosis strained the family's emotional and financial resources, and Rowling's relationship with her father was often tense. To escape, she retreated to her bedroom and the comfort of her books. Reading transported her to worlds far beyond the small village where she lived in the south of England. Asked about advice for aspiring writers, Rowling later told an interviewer, "The most important thing is to read as much as you can, like I did. It will give you an understanding of what makes good writing and it will enlarge your vocabulary."

Rowling continued reading voraciously into her adulthood. At Exeter University, she had to pay a £50 library fine for having so many overdue books. (Her official biography credits her college reading of Latin classics with helping her create the spells in *Harry Potter*.)

Rowling, like all creative geniuses, engaged in intense consumption that gave her the raw ingredients for her own future creativity.

These ingredients all came together in the Harry Potter series. While each book has its own plot structure, the overall series follows a traditional rags-to-riches arc. Potter, the young orphan, doesn't even have a bed to sleep on. But by the end of the series, he has slain his nemesis, fallen in love, and is set to live happily ever after. Rowling took a traditional and familiar story structure—the orphan rising to greatness—and added her own twist: young wizards who are grappling with the complexities of growing up.

Iterations: Creating a World

J. K. Rowling got off the train when it reached London, feeling inspired.

If she had believed in the inspiration theory of creativity, she might have gone home and sat at her desk, waiting for yet more revelations.

Instead, inspired by the vision she'd already mapped out in her head, she began planning her books methodically. Rowling spent the next five years engaged in creative iterations, developing the plots of all seven books, and writing the first book.

Her story is *not* one of sudden inspiration leading to overnight success. In fact, Rowling is one of the most organized and driven fiction writers I found in my research. Once, during a television interview, she showed a journalist her papers. Among the troves of boxes were *fifteen* variations of the first chapter of book one alone, as well as a chart that included every single character in Harry Potter's class at Hogwarts that Rowling used to develop her plots.

It didn't stop here. Rowling published on her website a plot table she created to plan her fifth book. On the left-hand side, she listed every chapter, followed by a column for each subplot, and a map that helped her organize how various plotlines would unfold throughout the book.

Her original agent, Christopher Little, described to me how obvious her planning was when the two of them first met. "What was quite extraordinary was that she had a very clear picture in her head of seven books," he said. "If you asked a question about a particular scene, where you go down a corridor, and you turn into the third door on the left, she knew what was in the first door and the second door on the left."

Rowling was more than just a visionary; she was also a voracious planner who exerted immense effort.

Community

As I wrote earlier, creative communities are critical for guiding creators down the rough road toward achievement. And Rowling was no exception.

At one point, Rowling, a single mother, decided to relocate to Edinburgh to be closer to her sister, Dianne. Rowling's brother-in-law had just opened a small café called Nicolson's. Soon Rowling could be found in one corner of the coffee shop, writing about witches and wizards, her baby, Jessica, having fallen asleep earlier in her carriage. This gave Rowling the quiet, focused time she needed to write.

That said, things weren't going all that well for Rowling. She had no money and was forced to go on public assistance, receiving £68 a week as she looked for a job. Before long, she found herself in a clinical depression and sought out a therapist.

Without the support of her family and the help of a therapist, would *Harry Potter* even have come to fruition?

In addition, Rowling relied on collaborators and promoters to turn her debut novel into what would later become the Harry Potter phenomenon. After writing *Harry Potter and the Sorcerer's Stone*, Rowling knew she needed a literary agent, and went to Edinburgh's Central Library to hunt down possible names. As she leafed through the pages of an agent directory, one name caught her attention: Christopher Little.

Rowling had always loved folklore and children's tales, and Little's name sounded like a character in a children's book. That afternoon, long before the days of e-mail, she sent off a precious copy of her first three chapters via Royal Mail.

For his part, Christopher Little tended to avoid children's books, but he was immediately enamored by the world Rowling had created. He wrote her back promptly, asking to read the rest of the manuscript. Once he read it, Little offered to represent her, Rowling agreed, and the agent got to work pitching publishers.

Before long, the responses started trickling in:

Too small of an audience . . .
Stories about orphans won't do well . . .
Too scary for a children's book . . .
It should be 30,000 words max . . .

By the end, twelve British publishers turned it down.

It was then that Barry Cunningham, an editor at the then-small children's division of Bloomsbury, read the manuscript, loved it, and called Little. He wanted to make an offer on the book.

But Little had a plan. As he put it, "I restricted their offer to very limited territories and one book." His instincts told him that Harry Potter had legs, and he didn't want to give away too much too soon for a small sum.

On a Friday afternoon, Little called Rowling to give her the news.

She was speechless to hear that she was about to become a published author.

Worried by her silence, Little asked her, "Are you all right? Are you still there?"

"Um, well, it's just that my lifelong dream has come true."

As Little remembers it, "She was absolutely over the moon."

Bloomsbury paid only £2,500 as an advance, which, I might add, gave the publisher one of the greatest returns in literary history.

Rowling had accomplished her dream. She had sold her first novel, but to do that she relied on a promoter, who helped her land a contract with a reputable publisher.

In her new editor, Barry Cunningham, she found another collaborator who understood the creative curve and the importance of marketing, an industry foreign to Rowling.

Cunningham began his publishing career as a "marketing associate" at Puffin Books, the children's imprint of Penguin Books. He assumed the job would entail organizing literary campaigns. Instead, he often found himself dressed in a giant costume as the imprint's adorable penguin mascot.

In costume, Cunningham would visit classrooms with authors like Roald Dahl. Spending time with children helped him realize what kids looked for in books: "What children love to read is a blend of familiarity and adventure. The unfamiliar and the comforting all at the same time." Cunningham's marketing experience made him stand out from other publishers, who'd spent their whole lives on the editorial side of things. When he first read the manuscript of *Harry Potter*, he recognized that the combination of familiarity and novelty made it a perfect book for children.

The success of Rowling's book may have seemed due to luck or happenstance, but it was actually the result of thoughtful processes. Christopher Little planned to wait until the book was published in England to sell it to an American publisher, as he expected to be able to create early hype in the British market.

He didn't know the half of it. In the wake of *Harry Potter*'s U.K. publication, the book found passionate early fans. Three thousand miles away, American publishers started to hear good things about the book.

The result was an auction involving six publishers that was finally won by Scholastic for $105,000.

The sale gave rise to a torrent of media attention. A single mother and part-time teacher had done the impossible! *The Herald*'s headline announced, "Book Written in Edinburgh Cafe Sells for $100,000." Rowling, it seemed, was her own rags-to-riches story. The resulting attention gave her book the kind of mainstream exposure that most writers pray for and seldom get. And before long, *Harry Potter* had turned into an empire.

Rowling didn't wait for ideas to strike her. Instead, she toiled for years to create something great. She planned, outlined, and developed reference materials, going through endless iterations and drafts to get her story and her characters just right. Along the way she faced both personal and economic challenges, but she was sustained by a creative community, including her agent, and the team at Bloomsbury, and continued to write.

In other words, Rowling followed the laws of creativity.

One of the things I love most about Rowling's story is the colossal gap between the public perception of her creative process and the reality.

She didn't *just* get struck by lightning.

She didn't win the creative lottery.

She spent many years of her life reading, planning, and writing, and the result, of course, was and is *Harry Potter*.

A Parting Note

When we're children, we are told all the time how creative we are. Teachers and parents encourage us to draw multicolored creatures, create characters and friends out of toys (or thin air), and transform blocks into magical towers that keep watch over our darkening bedrooms.

But as we get older, that creative child inside us fades. In school, we learn how to take standardized tests and do trigonometry. We watch movies and read magazines that tell us stories of unattainable genius. Journalists package and sell creativity as the exclusive province of a rarefied few.

By the time we start considering a career, we've lost the images of ourselves as creative people. Instead, creative success becomes something abstract and distant. Something to read about, and perhaps desire, but seldom to take action on.

Two years ago, when I first began researching creativity, I came face-to-face with any number of conflicting stories, theories, and myths. What's more, even creative people whose careers would seem to encapsulate success found it hard to identify the roots of their creativity.

The mythology around stories like Rowling's makes creative success sound like a combination of good, even excessive, fortune and divine will. Easy for some, impossible for most. For many, these made-up stories of genius can be discouraging. By celebrating the greatness of very few, our culture signals that the rest of us either *have* it or *don't* have it.

But as I spoke to more and more creative artists in all industries, from all walks of life, patterns began to emerge of which few if any of the people I interviewed were aware: They were all doing the *same* things to spark and execute their creative ideas.

The final pieces fell into place when I met with researchers and academics, and became aware of the creative curve, the bell-shaped relationship between exposure and likability. This, I realized, is a fundamental mechanism underlying how trends come in and out of favor.

The world's best-known creative people follow a consistent pattern of behavior that allows them to create movies, novels, music, food, paintings, gadgets, and companies that hit the sweet spot on the creative curve.

Via relentless consumption, they planted the seeds for moments of sudden inspiration that could change the world with familiar—but not *excessively* familiar—ideas.

Through imitation, they learned the necessary constraints and formulas of their industries, and learned how to apply the precisely necessary amount of novelty.

Through building communities, they refined their skills, gained motivation, and found collaborators to help them execute their projects.

Finally, by being aware of timing and engaging in iterations, they took advantage of data and process to improve their work and achieve the ideal point of familiarity and novelty.

Creative success, in fact, is learnable, whether you're a starving artist or the head of an advertising firm.

And this is where I worry.

The fact that there's a pattern out there does *not* mean it's easy.

In fact, mastering the creative curve can take years.

In your hands is *not* a book telling you that with minimal effort you can be the next Mozart or Picasso, Elon Musk or J. K. Rowling.

No, this is a book that tells you that if you *choose* to dedicate your life to creativity, there *is* a path, and a set of key considerations you need to bear in mind, and need to *do*, to make success happen.

The laws of the creative curve provide a blueprint for how every one of us can unlock our creative potential. The patterns of creative success can be learned and, with time, mastered.

Of course, that gives you one less excuse for waiting until

tomorrow to begin writing that novel, setting down the lyrics to that song, or building that start-up.

Achieving your creative potential isn't for the faint of heart. It requires countless hours, days, and even years of work. But it's no longer a mystery.

Acknowledgments

I
f I had any doubts that the concept of a "lone creator" was a tall tale, writing a book dispelled them. There may be one name on the cover, but a book is a group effort. From the dozens of people who let me borrow their time to interview them, to the team that supported me through it, to the friends who read countless drafts, and, of course, to the folks at Crown who put it all together. Writing this book was one of the least individual things I've done.

There is a whirlwind of people who contributed to this. Trever gave me time and space to write and the feedback and encouragement I needed. Shane Snow was the first person to hear about the book, and his early encouragement and support directly led to my pursuing it. Shane is kind and wise and will be the author of many more great books over his career. He also introduced me to my future agent, Jim Levine, and generously gave me the idea for the Franklin method.

Jim is a sherpa more than an agent. His advice shaped the proposal and the eventual book. I am eternally grateful to him for putting me under his wing and taking a chance on a first-time author. His entire team made me feel like family (thanks, Matthew!).

He also connected me with the team at Crown and my excellent editor, Roger Scholl, who knows just where to push to make something great. I appreciate the entire team at Crown for taking a risk on me. It was always an ambition of mine to write a book and you made the process approachable. Thank you for putting up with all my questions.

Countless friends provided feedback for this book or supported it in other ways. Thanks to Dan Morse for his constant support and compassion. Peter Smith for his motivation and wisdom. Eric Kuhn for always having my back. Jack Barrow for countless edits and sage advice. Steve Loflin for being my original believer eight years ago. Susanna Quinn for being my third big sister. Joe Chernov, who shaped more of the proposal than he realizes.

My two research assistants, Steven Kelly and Nicole Brinkley, made it possible to actually write a book while having a full-time job. I could not have imagined doing this without their help in keeping me organized and finding things I needed. They are both brilliant and will both write bestselling books someday soon. Also, Bryan Wish has played a huge role in helping develop the audience that hopefully will read this book.

Greg Fisk, who was an amazing part of the team. His illustrations helped the book come alive in a way that wouldn't be possible with words alone. As they say, a picture is worth . . .

Rodrigo Corral, who truly made the cover worth looking at.

My father, who has become my writing buddy as he pursues a new career in fiction writing, was a constant source of support and advice. Even if my books have fewer UFOs than his, he was the best pen pal a new writer could ask for.

My mother, who loves me and shaped who I am today. I owe my curiosity to her and this book is a direct product of those early lessons.

My stepmother, who was a source of support and love throughout this process.

Numerous people provided interviews that didn't make the book but shaped many of the concepts in it. I am grateful that they lent me their time and am sorry I couldn't include them directly in the book.

The team at TrackMaven, who gave me the support to spend nights and weekends getting this done over the last two years, especially Tim, one of the best co-conspirators a man could ask for.

My board members at TrackMaven, who have taught me more about the workings of the professional world than I could ever have imagined (and I know I have so much more still to learn). I am the grateful recipient of the generous support and advice of people who have come before me. Joe, Sean, Chuck, Dan, and Patrick, I know I sometimes take you for granted and I thank you for not holding it against me. All of you have shaped who I am not only as a CEO but as a person. You have all shared with me way more wisdom than I deserve.

And of course, to Harry who gave me my first "big break" and believed in me in a way I could never fully internalize. I miss you so much and wish you could have read this. You were a wonderful father and husband and I aspire to live up to the standard you set. Also, I promise to be just as hard-working as you would have wanted me to be (except I probably won't call people while jogging).

To the wonderful coffee shops of D.C. where I wrote this, including Slipstream, Tryst, Compass Coffee, Colony Club, Emissary, Cove, Songbyrd, and the National Portrait Gallery Courtyard Café. Sorry for being that guy who sat there for way too long.

Finally, thanks to all my friends and family who put up with me being not as present over the last couple of years as I should have been. I appreciate your sticking with me during this time.

A Note on Sourcing and Methods

This book relies heavily on interviews with a great number of people. Practitioners of creativity gave me countless hours of their time to explain their processes to me. These interviews were always recorded and transcribed. Throughout the book, quotes are edited for clarity. No changes were made to the substance of a quote without approval from the interviewee.

In some stories or scenes, I relied on composites from multiple sources. Whenever possible, that was through primary sources (such as the interviews with J. K. Rowling's first publisher and agent). Sometimes this was from multiple external accounts.

The story of the critical reaction to *The Last Judgement* is based on accounts from Vasari. He had written multiple versions of the story, each with slightly different details. In this book, I used details from his multiple accounts and those of others to try to piece together a story that did not have gaps.

In the London cab study, I was not able to get more information about the participants and I used a fictional character named Saul to explain how the study worked. The ways in which he was recruited were dramatized, but the findings were not changed.

Finally, a fact-checker went through the book. Whenever possible, I also had academics or practitioners fact-check sections. This proved incredibly valuable and I am grateful for the time they all put into it. At the end of the book you'll find notes for the main substance and findings of the book.

Notes

Chapter 1

3 **Paul McCartney woke up obsessed:** Details relating to McCartney's "Yesterday" conception story drawn mostly from *The Beatles Anthology* (New York: Chronicle Books, 2000); Ray Coleman, *McCartney: Yesterday and Today* (London: Boxtree, 1995); Phillip McIntyre, "Paul McCartney and the Creation of 'Yesterday': The Systems Model in Operation," *Popular Music* 25 (2) (2006); David Thomas, "The Darkness Behind the Smile," *The Telegraph*, August 19, 2004; Alice Vincent, "Yesterday: The Song That Started as Scrambled Eggs," *The Telegraph*, June 18, 2015, http://www.telegraph.co.uk/culture/music/the-beatles/11680415/Yesterday-the-song-that-started-as-Scrambled-Eggs.html.

3 **Wimpole Street:** Details relating to McCartney's stay at Wimpole Street and the creation of "Yesterday" drawn from "People: Jane Asher," *The Beatles Bible* (date unlisted), https://www.beatlesbible.com/people/jane-asher/; Coleman, *McCartney*;

McIntyre, "Paul McCartney and the Creation of 'Yesterday'";
Thomas, "The Darkness Behind the Smile."

3 **It has been played:** Sean Magee, *Desert Island Discs: 70 Years of Castaways* (London: Transworld Publishers, 2012).

4 **is the fourth-highest:** "The Richest Songs in the World," BBC Four, 2012.

4 **"When you ask creative":** Gary Wolf, "Steve Jobs: The Next Insanely Great Thing," *Wired*, February 1, 1996, https://www.wired.com/1996/02/jobs-2/.

9 **The most enlightening theory:** Ian Hammond, "Old Sweet Songs: In Search of the Source of 'I Saw Her Standing There' and 'Yesterday,'" *Soundscapes: Journal on Media Culture* 5 (July 2002), http://www.icce.rug.nl/~soundscapes/VOLUME05/Oldsweet songs.shtml; and McIntyre, "Paul McCartney and the Creation of 'Yesterday.'"

Chapter 2

13 **Since its founding:** For more about TrackMaven, check out https://trackmaven.com/.

13 **Another study found:** "Annuitas B2B Enterprise Demand Generation Survey 2014," Annuitas (2014), http://go.bright talk.com/ANNUITAS_B2B_Enterprise_Demand-Generation _Download.html.

15 **A recent global study of five thousand:** "Adobe State of Create," Adobe 2012, http://www.adobe.com/aboutadobe/ pressroom/pdfs/Adobe_State_of_Create_Global_Benchmark _Study.pdf.

18 **In his 1967 book:** Morse Peckham, *Man's Rage for Chaos* (New York: Schocken Books, 1967).

18 **Almost fifty years later:** Jonah Berger, *Invisible Influence* (New York: Simon & Schuster, 2016); and Derek Thompson, *Hit Makers* (New York: Penguin, 2017).

Chapter 3

21 ***Amadeus* depicts Wolfgang Amadeus Mozart's:** Miloš Forman, *Amadeus* (The Saul Zaentz Company, 1984).

22 **Famed movie critic:** Roger Ebert, "Great Movie: Amadeus," RogerEbert.com, April 14, 2002, http://www.rogerebert.com/reviews/great-movie-amadeus-1984.

23 **This letter became a cornerstone:** Details relating to the letter drawn from Kevin Ashton, "Divine Genius Does Not Exist: Hard Work, Not Magical Inspiration, Is Essence of Creativity," *Salon*, February 1, 2015, http://www.salon.com/2015/02/01/divine_genius_does_not_exist_hard_work_not_magical_inspiration_is_essence_of_creativity/.

23 **It was a forgery:** William Stafford, *The Mozart Myths: A Critical Reassessment* (Redwood City: Stanford University Press, 1993).

23 **In reality, Mozart worked:** Details relating to Mozart's real life and productivity style drawn from "Wolfgang Mozart," *Biography.com*, https://www.biography.com/people/wolfgang-mozart-9417115; and David P. Schroeder, "Mozart's Compositional Processes and Creative Complexity," *Dalhousie Review* 73 (2) (1993), https://dalspace.library.dal.ca/bitstream/handle/10222/63147/dalrev_vol73_iss2_pp166_174.pdf?sequence=1; and "Biography of Wolfgang Amadeus Mozart," http://www.wolfgang-amadeus.at/en/biography_of_Mozart.php.

24 **Mozart even used a type of shorthand:** Ulrich Konrad, *Mozart's Sketches* (Oxford: Oxford University Press, 1992).

24 **original concerto:** Phillip McIntyre, *Creativity and Cultural Production: Issues for Media Practice* (New York: Palgrave Macmillan, 2012); and Robert Spaethling, *Mozart's Letters, Mozart's Life: Selected Letters* (New York: W. W. Norton & Company, 2000).

25 **Per la ricuperata salute:** "Mozart and Salieri 'Lost' Composition Played in Prague," BBC News, February 16, 2016, http://www.bbc.com/news/world-europe-35589422; and Sarah Pruitt, "Mozart's 'Lost' Collaboration with Salieri Performed in Prague," History Channel, February 17, 2016, http://www.history.com/news/mozarts-lost-collaboration-with-salieri-performed-in-prague.

25 **in a 2016 piece about creativity:** David Brooks, "What Is Inspiration?" *New York Times*, April 15, 2016, https://www.nytimes.com/2016/04/15/opinion/what-is-inspiration.html.

25 **Ph.D. dissertations:** Lucille Wehner et al., "Current Approaches Used in Studying Creativity: An Exploratory Investigation," *Creativity Research Journal*, January 1991, http://www.tandfonline.com/doi/abs/10.1080/10400419109534398.

26 **"A poet is a light":** Plato, *The Collected Dialogues of Plato* (Princeton: Princeton University Press, 1961).

26 **In fact, the word:** "mimesis," Merriam-Webster Online Dictionary, https://www.merriam-webster.com/dictionary/mimesis.

26 **Plato expanded:** McIntyre, *Creativity and Cultural Production*.

26 **The Latin term for genius:** Anna-Teresa Tymieniecka, *The Poetry of Life in Literature* (Dordrecht: Springer Netherlands, 2000).

27 **Aristotle, too, picks up this same refrain:** Walter Scott, "Review: The Man of Genius by Cesare Lombroso," *The Spectator*, 1892.

28 **However, according to Deborah Haynes:** Deborah J. Haynes, *The Vocation of the Artist* (New York: Cambridge University Press, 1997).

28 **A Vatican official was aghast:** Details relating to the tiff between Biagio and Michelangelo drawn mostly from William D.
Montalbano, "It's 'Judgment' Day for Unveiled Sistine Chapel,"
Los Angeles Times, April 9, 1994, http://articles.latimes.com/1994
-04-09/news/mn-43912_1_sistine-chapel; and Norman E. Land,
"A Concise History of the Tale of Michelangelo and Biagio da
Cesena," *Source: Notes in the History of Art* 32 (14) (Summer 2013),
https://www.academia.edu/11448286/A_Concise_History_of
_the_Tale_of_Michelangelo_and_Biagio_da_Cesena.

29 **Michelangelo was incensed by Biagio's criticism:** Details
relating to Vasari's literary exploits drawn mostly from Giorgio Vasari, *Lives of the Most Eminent Painters Sculptors and Archi-
tects*, translated by Gaston du C. de Vere (Project Gutenberg,
2008), https://www.gutenberg.org/files/25326/25326-h/25326
-h.htm#Page_xiii; and Alan G. Artner, "The Excellence of
Italian Drawing," *Chicago Tribune*, June 19, 1994, http://articles
.chicagotribune.com/1994-06-19/entertainment/9406190328
_1_disegno-giorgio-vasari-artists-and-craftsmen.

30 **The poet Philip Sidney:** Sir Philip Sidney, "The Defence of
Poesy" (1583).

30 **"The lunatic, the lover":** William Shakespeare, *A Midsummer
Night's Dream* (1595).

30 **"We will each write":** Details relating to Shelley's *Frankenstein* drawn mostly from Mary Shelley, *Frankenstein* (Mineola,
N.Y.: Dover Publications, 1994); "Mary Shelley," Biography
.com (date unlisted), https://www.biography.com/people/mary
-shelley-9481497; and "Mary Wollstonecraft Shelley," *Encyclopedia Britannica* (date unlisted), https://www.britannica.com/
biography/Mary-Wollstonecraft-Shelley.

32 **books that captured mainstream attention:** These books
are Francis Galton, *Hereditary Genius* (New York: Macmillan
and Co., 1892), http://galton.org/books/hereditary-genius/text/

pdf/galton-1869-genius-v3.pdf; Lombroso, *Man of Genius* (New York: Charles Scribner's Sons, 1896), http://www.gutenberg.org/ebooks/50539; and John Ferguson Nisbet, *The Insanity of Genius and the General Inequality of Human Faculty: Physiologically Considered* (Ward & Downey, 1891), https://archive.org/details/insanityof-genius00nisb.

33 **the Terman family:** Details relating to the life and works of Lewis Terman drawn mostly from Henry L. Minton, *Lewis M. Terman* (New York: New York University Press, 1988); Mitchell Leslie, "The Vexing Legacy of Lewis Terman," *Stanford Magazine* (2009), https://barnyard.stanford.edu/get/page/magazine/article/?article_id=40678; and Carl Murchison, *Classics in the History of Psychology* (Worcester, Mass.: Clark University Press, 1930), http://psychclassics.yorku.ca/Terman/murchison.htm.

35 **first IQ test:** Trisha Imhoff, "Alfred Binet," Muskingum University, 2000, http://muskingum.edu/~psych/psycweb/history/binet.htm.

35 **In 1916, believing that:** Lewis Madison Terman, *The Measurement of Intelligence* (Boston: Houghton Mifflin, 1916).

36 **he supported the sterilization:** Ann Doss Helms and Tommy Tomlinson, "Wallace Kuralt's Era of Sterilization," *Charlotte Observer*, September 26, 2011, http://www.charlotteobserver.com/news/local/article9068186.html.

36 **In 1921, he assembled:** Details relating to the Termites drawn mostly from Daniel Goleman, "75 Years Later, Study Still Tracking Geniuses," *New York Times*, March 7, 1995, http://www.nytimes.com/1995/03/07/science/75-years-later-study-still-tracking-geniuses.html?pagewanted=all; and Richard C. Paddock, "The Secret IQ Diaries," *Los Angeles Times*, July 30, 1995, http://articles.latimes.com/1995-07-30/magazine/tm-29325_1_lewis-terman.

37 **The successful group:** Leslie, "The Vexing Legacy of Lewis Terman."

Chapter 4

39 **divergent thinking ... is correlated:** Robert McCrae, "Creativity, Divergent Thinking, and Openness to Experience," *Journal of Personality and Social Psychology* 52 (6) (1987), http://psycnet.apa.org/journals/psp/52/6/1258/.

39 **Researchers in Austria wanted:** Emanuel Jauk, Mathias Benedek, Beate Dunst, and Aljoscha C. Neubauer, "The Relationship Between Intelligence and Creativity: New Support for the Threshold Hypothesis by Means of Empirical Breakpoint Detection," *Frontiers in Psychology* 41 (4) (July 2013), https://www.ncbi.nlm.nih.gov/pmc/articles/PMC3682183/. There is an additional paper that could be written on the nuances of this study. For example, the researchers also found that IQ and creative achievement are correlated up to a higher level than potential. Could that be because people with high IQ are more likely to identify the social and group dynamics necessary to create hits?

40 **This is what scientists call:** For more on this, see James Clear, "Threshold Theory: How Smart Do You Have to Be to Succeed?," *Huffington Post*, January 13, 2015, http://www.huffingtonpost.com/james-clear/threshold-theory-how-smar_b_6147954.html.

41 **Hardesty reminds me:** Details relating to Hardesty's life drawn mostly from my interviews with him.

43 **To get honest feedback:** See Hardesty's original thread here: http://www.conceptart.org/forums/showthread.php/870-Journey-of-an-Absolute-Rookie-Paintings-and-Sketches.

45 **One study looked at:** K. Anders Ericsson, "Deliberate Practice and the Modifiability of Body and Mind: Toward a Science of the Structure and Acquisition of Expert and Elite Performance," *International Journal of Sport Psychology* 38 (1) (2007), http://drjj5hc4fteph.cloudfront.net/Articles/2007%20IJSP%20-%20Ericsson%20-%20Deliberate%20Practice%20target%20art.pdf.

45 **Another study found that:** Robyn Dawes, *House of Cards* (New York: Free Press, 1996).

45 **One researcher compared:** James J. Staszewski, *Expertise and Skill Acquisition: The Impact of William G. Chase* (New York: Psychology Press, 2013).

45 **Another study evaluated:** Adriaan de Groot, *Thought and Choice in Chess* (New York and Tokyo: Ishi Press, 2016).

45 **Researchers found the importance:** Ericsson, "Deliberate Practice and the Modifiability of Body and Mind."

46 **One study that looked:** Mihaly Csikszentmihalyi, *The Systems Model of Creativity: The Collected Works of Mihaly Csikszentmihalyi* (Dordrecht: Springer Netherlands, 2014).

47 **This training has origins from:** Juliette Aristides, *Classical Drawing Atelier* (New York: Watson-Guptill Publications, 2006).

49 **K. Anders Ericsson:** Details relating to Ericsson and "purposeful practice" drawn from K. Anders Ericsson, Ralf Th. Krampe, and Clemens Tesch-Romer, "The Role of Deliberate Practice in the Acquisition of Expert Performance," *Psychological Review* 100 (3) (July 1993), http://www.nytimes.com/images/blogs/freako nomics/pdf/DeliberatePractice(PsychologicalReview)pdf; my interviews with him; Neil Charness, "The Role of Deliberate Practice in Chess Expertise," *Applied Cognitive Psychology* 19 (2) (March 2005); and Ericsson, "Deliberate Practice and the Modifiability of Body and Mind."

50 **the power of purposeful practice:** That study is Ericsson et al., "The Role of Deliberate Practice in the Acquisition of Expert Performance."

52 **Classical Art Online:** Find that site here: http://www.classical artonline.com/.

53 **Saul was a London cabbie:** Eleanor A. Maguire, Katherine Woollett, and Hugo J. Spiers, "London Taxi Drivers and Bus

Drivers: A Structural MRI and Neuropsychological Analysis," *Hippocampus* 16 (12) (2006).

56 **Studies have shown:** Aneta Pavlenko, "Bilingual Cognitive Advantage: Where Do We Stand?," *Psychology Today* blog, November 12, 2014, https://www.psychologytoday.com/blog/life -bilingual/201411/bilingual-cognitive-advantage-where-do-we -stand.

56 **One study found that training:** K. Ball et al., "Effects of Cognitive Training Interventions with Older Adults: A Randomized Controlled Trial," *Journal of the American Medical Association* 288 (18) (November 13, 2002), https://www.ncbi.nlm.nih.gov/ pubmed/12425704.

56 **Another study found that ten 60-minute:** Joyce Shaffer, "Neuroplasticity and Clinical Practice: Building Brain Power for Health," *Frontiers in Psychology* 7 (July 26, 2016), https://www.ncbi .nlm.nih.gov/pmc/articles/PMC4960264/.

56 **To find out, I spoke to Joyce Shaffer:** Details relating to brain plasticity drawn mostly from my interviews with Joyce Shaffer.

56 **According to one study:** Dan Cossins, "Human Adult Neurogenesis Revealed," *The Scientist,* June 7, 2013, http://www.the -scientist.com/?articles.view/articleno/35902/title/human-adult -neurogenesis-revealed/.

Chapter 5

59 **Charles Darwin was panicked:** Details relating to Alfred Wallace and Charles Darwin drawn mostly from "Charles Darwin," *Encyclopedia Britannica* (2017), https://www.britannica.com/bi -ography/Charles-Darwin; "Alfred Russel Wallace," *Encyclopedia Britannica* (2017), https://www.britannica.com/biography/ Alfred-Russel-Wallace; "Charles Darwin," Famous Scientists (2017), https://www.famousscientists.org/charles-darwin/; and

"Biography of Wallace," Wallace Fund, 2015, http://wallace fund.info/content/biography-wallace; "He Helped Discover Evolution, and Then Became Extinct," *Morning Edition*, NPR, April 20, 2013, http://www.npr.org/2013/04/30/177781424/he -helped-discover-evolution-and-then-became-extinct.

60 **he traveled the world on the *Beagle*:** Charles Darwin, *The Voyage of the* Beagle (New York: Penguin, 1989).

61 **June 18, 1858:** Read that letter here: http://www.rpgroup .caltech.edu/courses/PBoC%20GIST/files_2011/articles/ Ternate%201858%20Wallace.pdf.

61 **Upon his return, Wallace published:** Wallace published the books *Palm Trees of the Amazon and Their Uses* and *Travels on the Amazon.*

62 **Darwin and Wallace had experienced:** For more on simultaneous invention, also known as multiple discovery, check out http://www.huffingtonpost.com/jacqueline-salit/a-multiple -independent-di_b_4904050.html.

62 **"And in the ages":** Lucretius, *Delphi Complete Works of Lucretius* (Delphi Classics, 2015).

63 **"But it is very far":** Charles Darwin, *The Works of Charles Darwin, Volume 16: The Origin of Species, 1876* (New York: New York University Press, 2010).

64 **One Darwin historian:** "Darwin's Theory of Evolution—Or Wallace's?" The Bryant Park Project, NPR, July 1, 2008, http:// www.npr.org/templates/story/story.php?storyId=92059646& from=mobile.

65 **"As a teenager I lived":** Mihaly Csikszentmihalyi, *The Systems Model of Creativity: The Collected Works of Mihaly Csikszentmihalyi* (Dordrecht: Springer Netherlands, 2014).

65 **He is known for his:** Mihaly Csikszentmihalyi, *Flow: The Psychology of Optimal Experience* (New York: Harper, 2008); and Mihaly

Csikszentmihalyi, "Flow, The Secret to Happiness," TED Talk, 2004, https://www.ted.com/talks/mihaly_csikszentmihalyi_on _flow.

65 **Csikszentmihalyi looks like:** Details relating to Csikszentmihalyi and his work drawn mostly from my interviews with him, Csikszentmihalyi, *The Systems Model of Creativity*; and Jacob Warren Getzels and Mihály Csíkszentmihályi, *The Creative Vision: A Longitudinal Study of Problem Finding in Art* (Hoboken, N.J.: Wiley, 1976).

Chapter 6

73 **According to the Social Security Administration:** "Get Ready for Baby," Social Security Administration (2017), https://www.ssa.gov/cgi-bin/babyname.cgi.

73 *The New York Times Magazine* **even ran an article:** Peggy Orenstein, "Where Have All the Lisas Gone?," *New York Times Magazine*, July 6, 2003, http://www.nytimes.com/2003/07/06/magazine/where-have-all-the-lisas-gone.html.

74 **During World War II:** Details relating to Zajonc's life and works drawn mostly from Margalit Fox, "Robert Zajonc, Who Looked at Mind's Ties to Actions, Is Dead at 85," *New York Times*, December 7, 2008, http://www.nytimes.com/2008/12/07/education/07zajonc.html.

74 **One critical experiment:** Robert B. Zajonc, "Attitudinal Effects of Mere Exposure" *Journal of Personality and Social Psychology* 9 (2) (June 1968), http://www.morilab.net/gakushuin/Zajonc _1968.pdf.

76 **Researchers Leslie Zebrowitz and Yi Zhang:** Details relating to Zebrowitz and Zhang's work drawn from interviews with Dr. Zhang.

77 **To find out, Dr. Zhang:** Leslie A. Zebrowitz and Yi Zhang, "Neural Evidence for Reduced Apprehensiveness of Familiarized Stimuli in a Mere Exposure Paradigm" *Social Neuroscience* 7 (4) (July 2012).

78 **Don Ed Hardy:** Details relating to the rise and fall of the Ed Hardy brand drawn mostly from "The 700 Lombard Street Shop Is the Third Incarnation of Tattoo City," Ed Hardy's Tattoo City (2011), http://www.tattoocitysf.com/history.html; and Matthew Schneier, "Christian Audigier, Fashion Designer, Dies at 57," *New York Times*, July 13, 2015, https://www.nytimes.com/2015/07/14/business/christian-audigier-57-fashion-designer.html.

79 **Hardy researched Audigier:** Jesse Hamlin, "Don Ed Hardy's Tattoos Are High Art and Big Business," *SFGate*, September 30, 2006, http://www.sfgate.com/entertainment/article/Don-Ed-Hardy-s-tattoos-are-high-art-and-big-2486891.php.

79 **The particular marketing strategy:** Margot Mifflin, "Hate the Brand, Love the Man: Why Ed Hardy Matters," *Los Angeles Review of Books*, August 25, 2013, https://lareviewofbooks.org/article/hate-the-brand-love-the-man-why-ed-hardy-matters/.

79 **That same year the Ed Hardy brand:** Mo Alabi, "Ed Hardy: From Art to Infamy and Back Again," CNN, September 30, 2013, http://www.cnn.com/2013/09/04/living/fashion-ed-hardy-profile/index.html.

79 **Another study conducted by Zajonc:** R. B. Zajonc et al., "Exposure, Satiation, and Stimulus Discriminability," *Journal of Personality and Social Psychology* 21 (3) (March 1972), https://www.ncbi.nlm.nih.gov/pubmed/5060747.

83 **Researchers at the University of Toronto:** E. Glenn Schellenberg, "Liking for Happy- and Sad-Sounding Music: Effects of Exposure" (Psychology Press, 2008), https://www.utm.utoronto.ca/~w3psygs/FILES/SP&V2008.pdf.

83 **Professor Glenn Schellenberg:** Details relating to Schellenberg's work drawn from my interviews with him.

84 **He told the *New York Post*:** Kristen Fleming, "That Inking Feeling," *New York Post*, June 16, 2013, https://nypost.com/2013/06/16/that-inking-feeling/.

85 **"That's what tanked it":** Ibid.

88 **In early 2004:** Details relating to the early days of Facebook and CampusNetwork drawn from Christopher Beam, "The Other Social Network," *Slate*, September 29, 2010, http://www.slate.com/articles/technology/technology/2010/09/the_other_social_network.html; Nicholas Carlson, "At Last—The Full Story of How Facebook Was Founded," *Business Insider*, March 5, 2010, http://www.businessinsider.com/how-facebook-was-founded-2010-3?op=1/#ey-made-a-mistake-haha-they-asked-me-to-make-it-for-them-2; and my interviews with Wayne Ting.

89 **"There is no community":** Jeremy Quach, "Throwback Thursday: Thefacebook vs. CampusNetwork," *Stanford Daily*, May 7, 2015, http://www.stanforddaily.com/2015/05/07/throwback-thursday-thefacebook-vs-campusnetwork/.

89 **Wayne Ting's start-up experience:** Details relating to CampusNetwork's failure and the success of Facebook drawn from my interviews with Ting and David Kirkpatrick.

89 **Looking back, Ting now:** Rory Cellan-Jones, "Wayne Ting, Nearly a Billionaire. Or How Facebook Won," *dot.Rory*, blog, BBC News, December 21, 2010, http://www.bbc.co.uk/blogs/thereporters/rorycellanjones/2010/12/wayne_ting_nearly_a_billionair.html.

90 **Zuckerberg is quoted as:** David Kirkpatrick, *The Facebook Effect* (New York: Simon & Schuster, 2011).

90 **explained during a lecture:** Watch that lecture here: https://www.youtube.com/watch?v=zCdTP2Hn26A.

92 **Dr. Düzel:** University College London, "Novelty Aids Learning," *Science Daily*, August 4, 2006, https://www.sciencedaily.com/releases/2006/08/060804084518.htm.

95 **Advertising researcher Christie Nordhielm:** Christie L. Nordhielm, "The Influence of Level of Processing on Advertising Repetition Effects," *Journal of Consumer Research* 29 (3) (December 2002).

96 **It was 1965:** Details relating to the Beatles' experimentation with the sitar drawn mostly from *The Beatles Anthology* (New York: Chronicle Books, 2000); and "The Beatles and India," The Beatles Bible (date unlisted), https://www.beatlesbible.com/features/india/.

97 **Shankar, on tour:** "Ravi Shankar: 'Our Music Is Sacred'—a Classic Interview from the Vaults," *The Guardian*, December 12, 2012, https://www.theguardian.com/music/2012/dec/12/ravi-shankar-classic-interview.

97 **Professor Tuomas Eerola:** Tuomas Eerola, "The Rise and Fall of the Experimental Style of the Beatles," *Soundscapes*, 2000, http://www.icce.rug.nl/~soundscapes/VOLUME03/Rise_and_fall3.shtml.

Chapter 7

103 **It was 1982:** Details relating to Ted Sarandos's early life drawn mostly from David Segal, "The Netflix Fix," *New York Times Magazine*, February 8, 2013, http://tmagazine.blogs.nytimes.com/2013/02/08/the-netflix-fix/; Dominique Charriau, "Ted Sarandos," *Vanity Fair* (date unlisted), http://www.vanityfair.com/people/ted-sarandos; and my interviews with him.

106 **acquired for $450 million:** Alyson Shontell, "German Publishing Powerhouse Axel Springer Buys Business Insider at a Whopping $442 Million Valuation," *Business Insider*, Septem-

ber 30, 2015, http://www.businessinsider.com/axel-springer -acquiresbusiness-insider-for-450-million-2015-9.

106 **acquired for $250 million:** Jason Del Rey, "Hudson's Bay Confirms $250 Million Acquisition of Gilt Groupe," *Recode*, 2016, https://www.recode.net/2016/1/7/11588582/hudsons-bay -confirms-250-million-acquisition-of-gilt-groupe.

106 **valued at over $1.5 billion:** Erin Griffith, "Kevin Ryan, the 'Godfather' of NYC Tech, on Serial Entrepreneurship, Gilt's IPO and a Possible Run for Mayor," *Fortune*, June 30, 2014, http:// fortune.com/2014/06/30/kevin-ryan-interview-gilt-groupe/.

106 **for over $1 billion:** Ibid.

106 **Another successful serial entrepreneur is:** Details relating to Rothblatt drawn from "Profile: Martine Rothblatt," *Forbes* (May 17, 2017), https://www.forbes.com/profile/martine -rothblatt/; and "How a Millionaire Saved Her Daughter's Life— and Tens of Thousands of Others in the Process," *Business Insider*, May 5, 2016, http://www.businessinsider.com/martine-rothblatt -saved-daughters-life-united-therapeutics-2016-5.

106 **over $25 billion:** "Sirius XM Holdings Inc," Google Finance (2017), https://www.google.com/finance?cid=821110323948726.

106 **over $5 billion:** "United Therapeutics Corporation," Google Finance (2017) https://www.google.com/finance?q=United+Therapeutics.

107 **Professor Robert Baron:** Robert A. Baron, "Opportunity Recognition as Pattern Recognition: How Entrepreneurs 'Connect the Dots' to Identify New Business Opportunities," *Academy of Management Perspectives*, February 2006, http://www.iedmsu.ru/ download/fa4_1.pdf.

107 **The answer, he found, is pattern recognition:** Ibid.

109 **Earlier I mentioned serial entrepreneur Kevin Ryan:** Quotes from Ryan drawn from my interviews with him.

112 **Ted Sarandos has continued to consume:** These details relating to Sarandos's professional life drawn mostly from my interviews with him.

114 **Connor Franta looks:** Details relating to Franta drawn from Libby Ryan, "Wipe Those Tears and Meet Connor Franta, Minnesota's YouTube Superstar," *Star Tribune*, April 30, 2015, http://www.startribune.com/wipe-those-tears-and-meet-minnesota-s-youtube-superstar/301705331; and my interviews with him.

117 **It's the setting of a classic psychology study:** Norman R. F. Maier, "Reasoning in Humans. II. The Solution of a Problem and Its Appearance in Consciousness," University of Michigan (August 1931).

121 **the researchers began dropping hints:** Mark Jung-Beeman et al., "Neural Activity When People Solve Verbal Problems with Insight," *PLOS Biology*, April 13, 2004, https://sites.northwestern.edu/markbeemanlab/files/2015/11/Neural-activity-observed-in-people-solving-verbal-problems-with-insight-1cspclw.pdf.

122 **Edward Bowden is a:** Edward M. Bowden and Mark Jung-Beeman, "Aha! Insight Experience Correlates with Solution Activation in the Right Hemisphere," *Psychonomic Bulletin and Review* 10 (3) (September 2003), http://groups.psych.northwestern.edu/mbeeman/pubs/PBR_2003_Aha.pdf.

128 **One survey:** "Shower for the Freshest Thinking," Hansgrohe Group (December 5, 2014), http://www.hansgrohe.com/en/23002.htm.

128 **Mike Einziger:** Details relating to Einziger drawn mostly from my interview with him; Anthony Ha, "With MIXhalo, Incubus Guitarist Mike Einziger Aims to Deliver Studio-Quality Sound at Live Events," *TechCrunch*, 2017, https://techcrunch.com/2017/05/17/with-mixhalo-incubus-guitarist-mike-einziger-aims-to-deliver-studio-quality-sound-at-live-events/; Marshall Perfetti, "Incubus Is Imperfect on First

Album in Six Years," *Cavalier Daily*, April 25, 2017, http://www
.cavalierdaily.com/article/2017/04/incubus-is-imperfect-on
-first-album-in-six-years; and my interviews with him.

129 **Working alongside a team of Italian researchers:** Carola
Salv et al., "Insight Solutions Are Correct More Often Than An-
alytic Solutions," *Thinking & Reasoning* 22 (4) (2016), https://sites
.northwestern.edu/markbeemanlab/files/2015/11/Salvi_etal
_Insight-is-right_TR2016-2n3ns9l.pdf.

Chapter 8

133 **Beverly Jenkins was nine:** Details relating to Jenkins's work
drawn from my interviews with her.

135 **Romance novels make up:** Statistics on romance novel industry from "Romance Statistics," Romance Writers of America
(date unlisted), https://www.rwa.org/page/romance-industry
-statistics.

135 **Sarah MacLean:** Read her monthly column here: http://www
.sarahmaclean.net/reviews/.

135 **For MacLean, this makes:** Details relating to MacLean's work
drawn from my interviews with her.

136 **Kurt Vonnegut wrote fourteen novels:** Details relating to
Vonnegut's life and work drawn mostly from "Kurt Vonnegut,"
Encyclopedia Britannica (2017), https://www.britannica.com/
biography/Kurt-Vonnegut.

136 **Unfortunately, he hated anthropology:** Kurt Vonnegut, *A
Man Without a Country* (New York: Seven Stories Press, 2005).

140 **brought together a team of academic superheroes:** The
study produced by his team of academic superheroes was Rea-
gan et al., "The Emotional Arcs of Stories Are Dominated by Six
Basic Shapes," EPJ Data Science, November 4, 2016, https://epj

datascience.springeropen.com/articles/10.1140/epjds/s13688
-016-0093-1.

142 **Kenya Barris:** Details relating to *Black-ish* and Barris's involvement and background drawn mostly from my interviews with
him.

144 **Researcher Gregory Berns:** Details relating to dopamine
drawn from my interviews with Berns.

144 **Berns was watching:** Take a listen: https://www.youtube.com/
watch?v=3wE5GBdPY30.

144 **Three years earlier, when he:** Details relating to Berns's search
drawn mostly from Gregory S. Berns and Sara E. Moore, "A Neural Predictor of Cultural Popularity," *Journal of Consumer Psychology* 22(1) (January 2012), https://www.cs.colorado.edu/~mozer/
Teaching/syllabi/TopicsInCognitiveScienceSpring2012/Berns
_JCP%20-%20Popmusic%20final.pdf; and my interviews with
him.

144 **Berns couldn't help but speculate:** Bianca C. Wittmann et
al., "Anticipation of Novelty Recruits Reward System and Hippocampus While Promoting Recollection," *Neuroimage* 38 (1)
(October 2007), https://www.ncbi.nlm.nih.gov/pmc/articles/
PMC2706325/.

146 **Alexis Ohanian had one goal:** Details relating to Ohanian and
his creation drawn mostly from Michelle Koidin Jaffee, "The
Voice of His Generation," *University of Virginia Magazine*, Fall 2014,
http://uvamagazine.org/articles/voice_of_his_generation; and
my interviews with him.

150 **a future American founding father:** Details relating to
Franklin's quest to improve his writing drawn mostly from Benjamin Franklin, *The Autobiography of Benjamin Franklin* (Project
Gutenberg, 2006), http://www.gutenberg.org/files/20203/20203
-h/20203-h.htm; and George Goodwin, "Ben Franklin Was

One-Fifth Revolutionary, Four-Fifths London Intellectual," *Smithsonian*, March 1, 2016, http://www.smithsonianmag.com/history/ben-franklin-was-one-fifth-revolutionary-four-fifths-london-intellectual-180958256/.

151 **He created the uber-popular:** Read that blog here: https://www.nytimes.com/by/andrew-ross-sorkin.

152 **connected over Skype:** Details relating to Sorkin's life and works drawn mostly from my interviews with him.

Chapter 9

156 **One study from the University of California:** D. K. Simonton, "The Social Context of Career Success and Course for 2,026 Scientists and Inventors," *Personality and Social Psychology Bulletin*, August 1, 1992.

156 **Another study found that a wide range:** Dr. Benjamin Bloom, *Developing Talent in Young People* (New York: Ballantine Books, 1985).

156 **Yet another study of successful artists:** D. K. Simonton, "Artistic Creativity and Interpersonal Relationships Across and Within Generations," *Journal of Personality and Social Psychology* 46 (6) (June 1984).

157 **Taylor Swift's album 1989:** "Taylor Swift," *Billboard* (date unlisted), http://www.billboard.com/artist/371422/taylor-swift/chart.

157 **You could call Martin:** Details relating to Martin drawn mostly from John Seabrook, "Blank Space: What Kind of Genius Is Max Martin?," *The New Yorker*, September 30, 2015, http://www.newyorker.com/culture/cultural-comment/blank-space-what-kind-of-genius-is-max-martin; and "List of Billboard number-one singles," Wikipedia (date unlisted), https://en.wikipedia.org/wiki/List_of_Billboard_number-one_singles.

157 **NPR once dubbed him:** "The Scandinavian Secret Behind All Your Favorite Songs," WBUR, 2015, http://www.wbur.org/onpoint/2015/10/02/dr-luke-taylor-swift-katy-perry-pop-music.

157 **Martin is in fact:** *Billboard* Staff, "Max Martin's Hot 100 No. 1s as a Songwriter—From Justin Timberlake's 'Can't Stop the Feeling!' to Britney Spears's '. . . Baby One More Time,'" *Billboard*, May 23, 2016, http://www.billboard.com/photos/7378263/max-martin-hot-100-no-1-hits-as-a-songwriter.

158 **Asked at a conference:** "Song Summit 2012: In Conversation—Arnthor Birgisson," Song Summit, YouTube, 2012, https://www.youtube.com/watch?v=i6jkDdc_b8I.

158 **Bonnie McKee is a lyricist:** Details relating to McKee drawn mostly from John Seabrook, "The Doctor Is In," *The New Yorker*, October 14, 2013, http://www.newyorker.com/magazine/2013/10/14/the-doctor-is-in.

159 **Back in the early 1980s:** Bloom, "Developing Talent in Young People."

160 **D. A. Wallach:** Details relating to Wallach's life and works drawn from Zack O'Malley Greenburg, "For 30 Under 30 Alum D. A. Wallach, a Strong Start to the Next 30," *Forbes*, November 24, 2015, https://www.forbes.com/sites/zackomalleygreenburg/2015/11/24/for-30-under-30-alum-d-a-wallach-a-strong-start-to-the-next-30/#18b4b49654bb; and my interviews with him.

160 **He also played:** He was one of the eighties singers at the daytime pool party.

161 **David Rubenstein:** Details relating to Rubenstein and the Carlyle Group drawn mostly from "About David," davidrubenstein.com (date unlisted), http://www.davidrubenstein.com/biography.html; "Profile: David Rubenstein," *Forbes*, October 10,

2017, https://www.forbes.com/profile/david-rubenstein/; and my interviews with him.

163 **Office space in the formerly rundown SoMa neighborhood:** Details drawn from "MarketBeat Manhattan Q1 2017," Cushman & Wakefield (2017), http://www.cushmanwakefield.com/en/research-and-insight/unitedstates/manhattan-office-snapshot/; "MarketBeat San Francisco Q1 2017," Cushman & Wakefield (2017), http://www.cushmanwakefield.com/en/research-and-insight/unitedstates/san-francisco-office-snapshot/; and "San Francisco," RedFin (2017), https://www.redfin.com/city/17151/CA/San-Francisco.

164 **Richard Florida:** Richard Florida, *The Rise of the Creative Class* (New York: Basic Books, 2014).

164 **In one study:** Brian Knudsen et al., "Urban Density, Creativity, and Innovation," *Creative Class*, May 2007, http://creativeclass.com/rfcgdb/articles/Urban_Density_Creativity_and_Innovation.pdf.

164 **This is the process:** For more on the knowledge spillover, see David B. Audretsch and Maryann P. Feldman, "Knowledge Spillovers and the Geography of Innovation," *Handbook of Urban and Regional Economics* 4 (May 9, 2003), http://www.econ.brown.edu/Faculty/henderson/Audretsch-Feldman.pdf.

166 **Brenda Chapman's mother:** Details relating to Chapman's life and works drawn mostly from Jim Vorel, "Lincoln Grad Proud of Her 'Brave' Oscar," *Herald & Review*, May 9, 2013, http://herald-review.com/entertainment/local/lincoln-grad-proud-of-her-brave-oscar/article_689eee72-b8e6-11e2-8919-0019bb2963f4.html; Nicole Sperling, "When the Glass Ceiling Crashed on Brenda Chapman," *Los Angeles Times*, May 25, 2011, http://articles.latimes.com/2011/may/25/entertainment/la-et-women-animation-sidebar-20110525; and my interviews with her.

168 **Benj Pasek is exuberant:** Details relating to Pasek and Paul drawn mostly from Michael Paulson, "What It's Like to

Make It in Showbiz with Your Best Friend," *New York Times*, November 10, 2016, http://nytimes.com/2016/11/13/theater/benj-pasek-justin-paul-dear-evan-hansen.html; Alexa Valiente, "'Dear Evan Hansen' Creators Benj Pasek and Justin Paul Say the Musical Almost Had a Different Storyline," ABC News, 2017, http://abcnews.go.com/Entertainment/dear-evan-hansen-creators-benj-pasek-justin-paul/story?id=47864862; Marc Snetiker, "First Listen: Dear Evan Hansen Debuts Inspiring Anthem 'You Will Be Found,'" *Entertainment Weekly* (January 30, 2017), http://ew.com/theater/2017/01/30/dear-evan-hansen-you-will-be-found-first-listen; and my interviews with Pasek.

170 ***Dear Evan Hansen* began its life:** That theater is Arena Stage in Washington, D.C.

170 **When *Dear Evan Hansen* premiered:** Charles Isherwood, "Review: In 'Dear Evan Hansen,' a Lonely Teenager, a Viral Lie and a Breakout Star," *New York Times*, December 4, 2016, https://www.nytimes.com/2016/12/04/theater/dear-evan-hansen-review.html.

172 **But for Hari Kondabolu:** Details relating to Kondabolu drawn mostly from my interviews with him.

172 ***The New York Times* calls him:** "Comedy Listings for July 29–Aug. 4," *New York Times*, July 28, 2016, https://www.nytimes.com/2016/07/29/arts/comedy-listings-for-july-29-aug-4.html.

173 **In 2003, Neistat uploaded:** Casey Neistat, "iPod's Dirty Secret - from 2003," YouTube, 2003, https://www.youtube.com/watch?v=SuTcavAzopg.

173 **HBO asked him:** "The Neistat Brothers," IMDb (date unlisted), http://www.imdb.com/title/tt1666727/.

173 **He posted his first videos:** Check him out! https://www.youtube.com/user/caseyneistat/videos

175 **Deller was a twenty-year-old:** Details relating to Deller drawn mostly from Alastair Sooke, "Jeremy Deller: 'When I

Got Close to Warhol,'" BBC, December 2, 2014, http://www.bbc
.com/culture/story/20141202-when-i-got-close-to-warhol.

176 **Mihaly Csikszentmihalyi:** Jacob Warren Getzels and Mihály
Csíkszentmihályi, *The Creative Vision: A Longitudinal Study of Problem Finding in Art* (Hoboken: Wiley, 1976).

178 **Maria Goeppert Mayer:** "Maria Goeppert Mayer—
Biographical," NobelPrize.org (date unlisted), https://www
.nobelprize.org/nobel_prizes/physics/laureates/1963/mayer
-bio.html; and "Maria Goeppert-Mayer," Atomic Heritage Foundation (date unlisted), http://www.atomicheritage.org/profile/
maria-goeppert-mayer.

178 **Harriet Zuckerman:** Harriet Zuckerman, *Scientific Elite: Nobel
Laureates in the United States* (New Brunswick: Transaction Publishers, 1977).

179 **In 2006, the country band:** CMT Staff, "Taylor Swift Joins
Rascal Flatts Tour," CMT News, 2006, http://www.cmt.com/
news/1543489/taylor-swift-joins-rascal-flatts-tour/.

180 **By 2015, Taylor Swift:** Christina Garibaldi, "Taylor Swift
Is Making Shawn Mendes' Dreams Come True," MTV News,
2014, http://www.mtv.com/news/1997360/taylor-swift-shawn
-mendes-1989-world-tour/.

180 **Researchers at New York University:** Andrea Gaggioli et
al., *Networked Flow: Towards an Understanding of Creative Networks*
(New York: Springer, 2013), http://www.springer.com/gp/
book/9789400755512.

180 **they studied the film credits:** Stacy L. Smith et al., "Inclu-
sion or Invisibility?," Annenberg School for Communication
and Journalism, February 22, 2016, http://annenberg.usc.edu/
pages/~/media/MDSCI/CARDReport%20FINAL%2022216
.ashx.

Chapter 10

185 **I'm sitting in a conference room:** Details relating to Ben & Jerry's drawn mostly from my interviews with Jerry Greenfield and with Ben & Jerry's staff, my visit to the headquarters, and first-tongue experience of the product. Also, from sources like "Our History," Ben & Jerry's (date unlisted), http://www.benjerry .com/about-us#1timeline.

199 **Nina Jacobson is one:** Details relating to Jacobson's life and works drawn mostly from my interviews with her.

199 **she is the founder:** Mike Fleming Jr., "'Hunger Games' Producer Nina Jacobson Acquires Kevin Kwan's 'Crazy Rich Asians,'" *Deadline*, August 6, 2013, http://deadline.com/2013/08/hunger -games-producer-nina-jacobson-acquires-kevin-kwans-crazy -rich-asians-557932/.

201 **Hollywood's quadrant approach:** For more, see Edward Jay Epstein, "Hidden Persuaders," *Slate*, July 18, 2005, http://www .slate.com/articles/arts/the_hollywood_economist/2005/07/ hidden_persuaders.html.

202 **Jon Penn:** Details relating to Penn's life and works drawn mostly from my interviews with him.

203 ***Fatal Attraction* went on:** "*Fatal Attraction*," IMDb (date un- listed), http://www.imdb.com/title/tt0093010/.

203 **Kevin Goetz:** Details relating to Goetz drawn mostly from my interviews with him and from "Who We Are," Screen Engine (date unlisted), http://www.screenenginellc.com/who.html.

205 **It's 1996. President Bill Clinton:** Bill Clinton, "Clinton's Speech Accepting the Democratic Nomination for President," *New York Times*, August, 30, 1996, http://www.nytimes.com/1996/08/30/ us/clinton-s-speech-accepting-the-democratic-nomination-for -president.html.

208 **By day, Heidi Joy Tretheway:** Details relating to Tretheway's life and works drawn mostly from my interviews with her.

Epilogue

213 **J. K. Rowling was stuck:** Details relating to Rowling's *Harry Potter* conception story drawn from "Harry Potter and Me," BBC, 2001, https://youtu.be/SrJiAG8GmnQ; Lindsay Fraser, "Harry and Me," *The Scotsman*, November 9, 2002, http://www.scotsman.com/lifestyle/culture/books/harry-and-me-1-628320; and "JK Rowling," Jkrowling.com (date unlisted), https://www.jkrowling.com/about/.

213 **as she later told *The New York Times*:** Doreen Carvajal, "Children's Book Casts a Spell Over Adults; Young Wizard Is Best Seller and a Copyright Challenge," *New York Times*, April 1, 1999, http://www.nytimes.com/1999/04/01/books/children-s-book-casts-spell-over-adults-young-wizard-best-seller-copyright.html.

214 **She never could have known that:** James B. Stewart, "In the Chamber of Secrets: J. K. Rowling's Net Worth," *New York Times*, November 24, 2016, https://www.nytimes.com/2016/11/24/business/in-the-chamber-of-secrets-jk-rowlings-net-worth.html.

214 **When pressed:** "Magic, Mystery, and Mayhem," Amazon.co.uk.

214 **"I [have] no idea":** "Magic, Mystery, and Mayhem: An Interview with J. K. Rowling," Amazon.co.uk (date unlisted), https://www.amazon.com/gp/feature.html?docId=6230.

214 **Her mother's multiple sclerosis:** Hayley Dixon, "JK Rowling Tells of Her Mother's Battle with Multiple Sclerosis," *The Telegraph*, April 28, 2014, http://www.telegraph.co.uk/news/celebritynews/10791375/JK-Rowling-tells-of-her-mothers-battle-with-multiple-sclerosis.html.

216 **Among the troves of boxes:** Details relating to Rowling's preparatory materials drawn from Rowling, "Harry Potter and Me."

216 **Rowling published on her website:** Find Rowling's hand-drawn plot sheet here: Colin Marshall, "How J. K. Rowling Plotted Harry Potter with a Hand-Drawn Spreadsheet," *Open Culture* (2015), http://www.openculture.com/2014/07/j-k-rowling -plotted-harry-potter-with-a-hand-drawn-spreadsheet.html.

216 **At one point, Rowling, a single mother:** Rachel Gillett, "From Welfare to One of the World's Wealthiest Women—The Incredible Rags-to-Riches Story of J. K. Rowling," *Business Insider,* May 18, 2015, http://www.businessinsider.com/the-rags -to-riches-story-of-jk-rowling-2015-5.

217 **She had no money:** Geordie Greig, "'I Was As Poor As It's Possible to Be . . . Now I Am Able to Give': In This Rare and Intimate Interview, JK Rowling Reveals Her Most Ambitious Plot Yet," *Daily Mail,* October 26, 2013, http://www.dailymail.co.uk/ home/event/article-2474863/JK-Rowling-I-poor-possible-be .html.

217 **Before long:** J. K. Rowling and Margaret Lenker, "5 Times J.K. Rowling Got Real About Depression," *The Mighty,* August 1, 2015, https://themighty.com/2015/08/5-times-j-k-rowling-got -real-about-depression/.

217 **one name caught her attention:** Details relating to Rowling's early work with Little drawn from Chris Hastings and Susan Bisset, "Literary Agent Made £15m Because JK Rowling Liked His Name," *The Telegraph,* June 15, 2003, http://www.telegraph.co .uk/news/uknews/1433045/Literary-agent-made-15m-because -JK-Rowling-liked-his-name.html; Fraser, "Harry and Me"; J. K. Rowling, "Harry Potter and Me," BBC, 2001, https://youtu.be/ SrJiAG8GmnQ; and David Smith, "Harry Potter and the Man Who Conjured Up Rowling's Millions," *The Guardian,* July 15, 2007, https://www.theguardian.com/business/2007/jul/15/har rypotter.books.

217 **By the end:** Alison Flood, "JK Rowling Says She Received 'Loads' of Rejections Before Harry Potter Success," *The Guardian*, March 24, 2015, http://www.foxnews.com/story/2008/03/23/jk-rowling-considered-suicide-while-suffering-from-depression-before-writing.html.

217 **It was then that Barry Cunningham:** Details relating to Cunningham's involvement drawn mostly from my interviews with him.

219 **The result was:** Lisa DiCarlo, "Harry Potter and the Triumph of Scholastic," *Forbes*, May 9, 2002, https://www.forbes.com/2002/05/09/0509harrypotter.html.

219 **"Book Written in Edinburgh Cafe":** "New Cafe at Building Where JK Rowling Penned Harry Potter Book," *The Scotsman*, October 31, 2009, http://www.scotsman.com/news/new-cafe-at-building-where-jk-rowling-penned-harry-potter-book-1-1222584; and "Book Written in Edinburgh Cafe Sells For $100,000," *The Herald* (1997).

Index

Page numbers in *italics* refer to illustrations.

About the Author

Allen Gannett founded and is the CEO of TrackMaven, a marketing data and intelligence service that has been used by some of the world's biggest brands, including General Electric, Microsoft, Marriott, Fidelity, and other Fortune 500 companies. TrackMaven is the leader in marketing, helping brands unlock the science of their social, content, and digital advertising by analyzing millions of pieces of marketing content and uncovering actionable insights. He is also an online contributor for *Fast Company*, where he writes about the intersection of the science and art of our digital lives.

He is an active technology investor, and previously cofounded and was a partner at Acceleprise Ventures, an early-stage venture capital fund that invests in software companies through an accelerator model.

He lives in Washington, D.C., with his mischievous four-year-old corgi.